MAKE
A DIFFERENCE

How to Share Your Faith in Christ as a Lifestyle

donSUNSHINE
m i n i s t r i e s
•until the whole world hears•

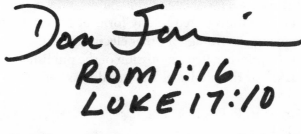

Don Fav
ROM 1:16
LUKE 17:10

DON SUNSHINE

ISBN 978-1-0980-5724-4 (paperback)
ISBN 978-1-0980-5725-1 (digital)

Christian Faith Publishing, Inc.
832 Park Avenue
Meadville, PA 16335
www.christianfaithpublishing.com

Printed in the United States of America

I would like to thank Ron Hutchcraft, who pressured me in October of 2004 to build the "Make a Difference" Live Event (M.A.D.) to equip people to share their faith in Christ as a lifestyle, as I had been doing. My thanks also go to my brother and friend, John Owens, General Manager of "The Light FM", Billy Graham's radio stations, for repeatedly encouraging me to write this book. My appreciation also goes to Cliff Springs with Genesis Studios in Cayce, SC for the cover design. And, lastly, my sincere thanks to my wife, Cathy, who is my partner in life and ministry. She diligently works to handle all of the behind the scenes things that need to get done…accounting, donor relations, support letters, cards, etc. I couldn't do the ministry that God has called me to without her. I love you, Cathy!

INTRODUCTION

My name is Don Sunshine. Yes, Sunshine is really my last name. Sunshine was a great name when I was in sales, but it was a terrible name when I was a police officer on a SWAT team in New Jersey!

I am not ordained. I don't have a seminary or Bible college degree. I am a layperson, and I am living proof that you don't need a bunch of specialized degrees to be able to share your faith in Christ every day as a lifestyle and begin making biblical disciples. My wife and I travel around the country teaching the body of Christ how to share their faith every day in obedience. As of this writing, I have completed over 640 events in twenty-seven states and Canada, equipping over 35,000 people to begin sharing their faith in Christ and making disciples. We have seen God use this simple training to change thousands of lives, and we've been blessed to see over 1,600 people actually get saved at the training, all to the glory of God!

We are a faith-based ministry. All we ask of churches is to cover our travel expenses and take a love offering to support our work. We don't require any minimums or financial guarantees. Whatever the Lord provides from the love offering is sufficient. The Make a Difference (MAD) Live Event is four hours of instruction, plus breaks. We usually do it on a Saturday or Sunday. Saturday would run from 9:00 a.m. to 2:30 p.m., with two breaks; one is for lunch. Sunday, we work around the church schedule. We don't do any role-playing or breaking up into groups to practice what I'm teaching. We provide a handout, and all the participants do is fill in the blanks as I teach. We'd love to come to your church and help equip the congregation. Please let me know if you'd like us to come! This book is a summary of what is taught in the live event, although not everything is included in the book. The live event features some very impactful videos and stories that help illustrate the truths that I am teaching.

Here's a question for you: how would your Christian life change if every day without fear, without embarrassment, without hesitation, you could naturally share your faith in Christ with one person? What if on some days it was two people? Or on some days five or more people? It's a whole lot easier to do than you've been led to believe.

We're going to cover three main parts in this book. The first one is, How do I recognize the opportunities that God gives me every day to share my faith but I miss them? What does it mean to be an ambassador for Jesus Christ? What are the fears that keep me from sharing my faith? I will show you how to beat those fears. Because unless we deal with the fears that stop us, nothing is going to change by reading this book. And lastly, what does it look like when the door opens for me to share my faith, and what do I do and say when the door opens?

We were created by God to go "MAD." That doesn't mean crazy, insane, or nuts. It means that God left us here to "make a difference." There are all kinds of differences that we can make in people's lives, but the most important difference you can ever make is to take someone to heaven with you. If you haven't been used yet by the God of the universe to change someone's eternal address, you don't know what you're missing! It energizes your entire Christian experience, and the Christian life becomes the great adventure that God intended it to be but very few of us get to experience.

After reading this book, I'm going to ask you to take a risk. It is not a big risk. What I am going to share with you is exactly what I teach in Christian middle schools and high schools around the country. It is so easy to do that I have the testimonies of the parents of two seven-year-olds who sat through this on a Sunday morning and put it into practice immediately. The first one was a young man named Lincoln. After the training, he was standing with his parents on his front lawn, and he told his mom and dad that he felt the Holy Spirit was prompting him to share Jesus with the neighbor across the street. They encouraged him to go and said they would pray for him as he shared. He went across the street and shared the Gospel with the neighbor.

Another young boy was sharing the Gospel with his fellow students on the school bus. He had led a number of these young people to Christ, and the family was buying Bibles for these new young believers. I have the testimony from the parents of a ten-year-old from the Valley Forge Baptist Temple in Pennsylvania. He took the training at his school and then again at his church. He used his allowance to purchase thirty Gospels of John and had his aunt, who was a missionary at home on furlough, take him to the train station so he could share the Gospels with the commuters. He didn't return home until he had shared with thirty people! This is much easier to do than you've been led to believe!

We are all familiar with the story of the Titanic. Allegedly, the ship was unsinkable. When it struck the iceberg over a hundred years ago, Captain Smith knew he had more lifeboats than required by law. But if he filled every single lifeboat to capacity, he knew that at least a thousand people were going to die that night, and there was nothing he could do to change that. He gave the order to load women and children first. Compounding the problem was that they never practiced lifeboat drills. They didn't believe they would ever need them, especially on a maiden voyage. The resulting chaos led to almost every single lifeboat being launched less than half full. I read reports from people who were in lifeboats that could've held forty people but were launched with only twelve people in them. Imagine for a moment that you're in a lifeboat with twenty-eight free seats. There's a mate assigned to your boat. He gives the order to start rowing away from the gigantic ship. You begin to row, and a short time later, the lifeboat naturally coasts to a stop. You do a little math and tell the mate that there are twenty-eight free seats in the lifeboat. You have three loved ones who are still on that ship! Why can't we go back and get them? That will still leave us room for twenty-five more people! The mate responds that we are not going back for anyone. Keep rowing. The lifeboat moves farther from the ship and naturally slows to a stop again. This time, you watch the nightmare of nightmares unfold. As this gigantic ship fills with water, the stern comes up out of the water, just like you saw in the movie. People were sliding down the decks and bouncing off things into the frigid ocean. Then you hear the deafening sound of water pressure ripping this gigantic ship in half. I think if you plugged your fingers in your ears, it was still painfully loud. This gigantic ship breaks into two pieces and disappears below the surface in two pieces, as if it had never existed.

About 328 people survive the sinking of the ship, and they are very much alive in the twenty-eight-degree saltwater. But they are not going to be alive for very long unless someone cares enough to go back and rescue them. And they are screaming, begging the people in the lifeboats to come back for them.

Only one lifeboat went back. They rescued six people. So 322 people are going to freeze to death because no one cares enough to go back for them. Imagine sitting in a lifeboat with twenty-eight free seats, and only a short distance in front of you are 322 people screaming for help. You and the rest of the people in your lifeboat sit still and make no effort to go back for them. Very quickly, the roar of people begins to get quiet. People are dying fifteen, seventy-five, two hundred at a time. Then there's that one last voice holding out, and it is silenced, and pardon the pun, but there is dead silence on the water, and you're left with your thoughts. Reportedly, no one said anything to each other in the lifeboats. They just sat there stunned.

Early the next morning, a ship called the Carpathia arrives and rescues everyone who is in lifeboats. They retrieve as many frozen bodies as they can find floating in the North Atlantic. They give you a stateroom and a change of clothes, and you get to take a hot shower to warm up. Then you have to stand in front of a mirror and look yourself in the eyes. How do you feel knowing you did absolutely nothing and you could've done something? I read that several people who survived in the lifeboats eventually committed suicide. They couldn't live with the guilt of knowing they had so many free seats in their lifeboats, yet they made no effort to go back for anyone. I believe the rest probably had nightmares for the rest of their lives. I mean how do you live with yourself knowing you did absolutely nothing and you could've done something?

Sadly, that's a picture of the church in America today. Those of us who know Jesus Christ are safe and secure in God's eternal lifeboats. He has placed us in a sea of lost and dying people. They're not screaming. Most of them don't even know that they're lost. And we're not going back for them. Because we're content to have lifeboat parties with everyone who's already saved! We have fellowship dinners, small groups, Sunday school picnics, and Bible studies. There's nothing wrong with these things. But God has placed each of us in a sea of lost and dying people. Some are friends, relatives, coworkers, neighbors, people we meet at the grocery store or sit next to on an airplane. And we're not going back for them! You see the problem is we have a bad definition of evangelism. The devil has lied to every one of us and told us not to invite these people into our lifeboats because if they refuse, we fail. And we don't want to feel like a failure. So we don't say anything! We can't cause the spiritual growth no matter how hard we try. The Bible says, "Paul planted, Apollo's watered, but only God can cause the growth!" So all God expects us to do, as followers of Jesus Christ, is to say, "Listen, pal. I care about you. And if you stay where you are, you're going to die. Why don't you climb in the lifeboat with me? Here's how you can get in." If you just do that, you're 100 percent successful! We just need to tell them they're in trouble and how to get out of the trouble and then leave the results to God. A better definition of *evangelism* is "Successful evangelism is simply taking the initiative to share Jesus Christ in the power of the Holy Spirit and leaving the results to God." It takes all of the pressure off us to know that we don't have to cause the growth.

Chuck Swindoll said, "We are not the Holy Spirit. God doesn't expect us to win souls to Christ. Without the mercy and movement of God's Spirit, no one can muster the faith to believe in salvation through Jesus Christ. We are completely incapable of managing hearers' responses to God's message! All we can do is share the hope of life through belief in Jesus Christ. The worst thing we can do is hide our hope from those who languish in despair. We must allow compassion to compel us to obediently share the gospel with others."

So here's a tough question: how many people have you personally cared enough about that you went back for them and invited them into your lifeboat in the past year? How many? How many in the past two years? Five years? Or more? Sadly, many of us are thinking really small numbers, and that needs to change. If we look at why Jesus came, the Scripture says there's one reason that Jesus traded a throne in heaven for a Roman cross. He came to "seek and to save what was lost" (Luke 19:10). If I put my hand up and claim to be a follower of Christ, and that's what my Master did, it should be what I am doing! But we're not doing it! Statistics say that nine out of ten people who profess to follow Christ never share their faith with anyone! Jesus Himself said in John 14:12, "I tell you the truth, anyone who has faith in me, will do what I have been doing." Yet we're not doing it. There's a huge disconnect in the church in America today. David Platt, in his book *Follow Me*, said, "Disciples of Jesus can't help but make disciples of all nations. If we truly believe Jesus's words and know Jesus' worth, then we are compelled to be part of this task. Following Jesus necessitates believing Jesus. And believing Jesus will naturally lead to proclaiming Jesus. Consequently, a privatized faith in a resurrected Christ is practically inconceivable. Yet privatized Christianity is a curse across our culture and church today."

Most of us are familiar with the Great Commission found in Matthew 28. Sadly, it is probably more accurately called the Great

Omission or the Great Suggestion because very few followers of Jesus Christ are actively trying to fulfill the commission. James 1:22 admonishes us, "But don't just listen to God's word. You must do what it says."

David Jeremiah beautifully defined what making disciples looks like. He said, "Disciples are made when new believers are taught the Word, led by example, then trained to transfer the faith to others." That is what we are all called to do, which begins with us telling someone about our faith in Christ. Think about this: if Jesus commanded His followers down through the centuries to go and make disciples and you choose to ignore that command for your whole life, when you stand before Him, do you really believe that you will hear the wonderful words, "Well done, my good and faithful servant"?

Let's look at a biblical picture of how to make this eternal difference. We'll go back to the Old Testament to see a man named Moses. Moses lived in a nasty place called the desert. Have you ever been to one? They are very hot. There's lots of sand and very few things growing. We have an awesome, creative God who has a sense of humor. Think about it, He made a donkey talk! So instead of sending an angel to flutter on down and talk to Moses, what does He do? He creates the one and only butane bush! This bush is engulfed in flames, but it's not being consumed! Well, that's rather unusual! Moses looked around and didn't see a man running off with a torch in his hand, nor did he see lightning strike this bush, so how did it start on fire? He goes over to examine it, and then God says something very important to Moses. The Lord said, "I have indeed seen the misery of my people in Egypt." Moses starts to get excited. God continues, "I have heard them crying out, and I am concerned about their suffering." Moses's excitement continues to build. God continues, "So I have come down to rescue them." Moses is now jumping for joy! God continues, "And now the cry of the Israelites has reached me, so now go. I am sending you." At this point, Moses's elation bubble bursts. He argues with God, telling God that He doesn't know him very well. Moses told the Lord that he stutters when he speaks, he's not a leader, and he begged God multiple times to send someone else. God said, "I know who you are Moses. I built you. I am coming down to rescue my people. So now go I am sending you!" I think it's really cool that the God of the universe in most cases chooses to use the regular, flawed, everyday people like you and me to accomplish great things for Him. In the same way that He wanted to rescue His chosen people of Jews, so He sent Moses to do it, He wants to rescue some people in your sphere of influence. So He's going to send you to do it! God has seen all of the lost people in your life: some are friends, relatives, coworkers, neighbors, people we meet at the store or at the gas station. He's summoning you to join Him in a rescue mission to save their lives.

Christians are scared to death of the term *witnessing*. When someone hears that their church is having evangelism training on Saturday and they look at their schedule and it is blank, they panic! They will call the dentist and beg for a root canal on Saturday because they would much rather be in the dental chair than sit in an evangelism training! That's why we won't use the term *witnessing* in this book. There's an equally biblical concept, that of being a spiritual rescuer. Our theme throughout this book will be rescuing people for eternity, and I want you to start to see yourself as a spiritual rescuer. It's helped change my life and tens of thousands of people's lives whom I've had the privilege of sharing this with.

On January 13, 1982, Ronald Reagan was president of the United States. Air Florida flight 90 was at National Airport, which we now call Reagan International Airport. It was headed for Tampa loaded with vacationers. A raging blizzard had hit the DC area, and they had closed the airport. But they had this one plane away from the gate, and they said rather than try to drag it through the snow back to the gate, let's just get this flight out of here. So they brought out the de-icing trucks, and they de-iced the plane. However, they hadn't finished clearing the runway yet. While they waited for the runway to be cleared, snow continued to fall on the plane. The snow turned to ice. Snow built up on top of the ice, and when they got the clearance to take off, they flew straight up the Potomac River which was the normal flight path from National Airport. The pilot and the copilot were straining at the controls trying to get the plane aloft. They couldn't get enough lift to clear the Fourteenth St. Bridge; so they slammed into the bridge during rush hour, crushed a bunch of commuter vehicles that were stopped on the bridge, dropped onto the frozen Potomac River, broke into three pieces, and sank to the bottom. Out of everyone on the plane, they were only six survivors. Four were female flight attendants, and two were male passengers. They bobbed to the surface between the chunks of ice in thirty-three-degree water. Everyone who saw the plane crash, including a young man named Lenny Skutnik, stopped to see what had happened. A flight attendant named Priscilla had surfaced and was struggling to stay afloat. A helicopter had dropped her a life ring, but she was unable to hang onto it and make it to shore. Lenny realized that she was going to die if he didn't do something. So he removed his coat and sweater and jumped into the frozen Potomac River. He swam out and rescued her! Two weeks later, Ronald Reagan was giving the State of the Union address, and he did something that no US president in history had ever done. In the middle of his address, he recognized Lenny's heroics, and all of Congress gave Lenny a standing ovation. That started a tradition that continues today. Every US president since Ronald Reagan and Lenny Skutnik would have everyday heroes in the gallery, and the president would tell their story and have them recognized by Congress and the nation. In fact, the name stuck. They call those everyday heroes recognized at the State of Union address the Skutniks today! You see, every day people like Lenny Skutnik, and like you and me, can become a hero when we become a rescuer. How would you like to be a hero in God's eyes? It says in the last chapter of the book of Daniel, "Those who lead many to righteousness will shine like the stars forever." Wow! That sounds like something every follower of Jesus Christ should aspire to. Who is someone in your life that you care about that is not going to happen? From this point on, everything we do should help equip you to rescue that person for eternity.

CHAPTER 1

Recognize Why You Are, Where You Are

How do we rescue people for eternity?

1.   Recognize why you are where you are.

Are you familiar with the story of Esther? She was the queen of Persia during the seventy years that the Jews were in captivity and exile in Babylon. There was a bad guy in the story named Haman, who hated the Jews. He especially hated one Jew who wouldn't bow down to him. His name was Mordecai. This greatly disturbed Haman, and a plot was hatched to kill all of the Jews and impale Mordecai on a pole at the top of an eight-story-high gallows. Word got to Mordecai, and he wasn't terribly excited. He sent a note to his relative Esther, the queen of Persia, telling her of the plan and asking her to do something about it. Esther knew that she couldn't just stroll out in front of the king anytime she wanted. She had to be summoned by the king, and the king hadn't summoned her in about thirty days. If she showed up without being summoned, she would likely be killed by the guards. Esther suggested that all of the Jews fast and pray for three days. At the end of three days, even if it meant she would die, she would go to the king. After three days, she put on her royal robe and strolled out to the edge of the king's court, and I believe her heart was beating out of her chest. She could die in the next several seconds. She stepped out where the king could see her,

15

and when he saw her, he invited her to the throne next to him. Over a couple of days, some lunches and maneuvering, Esther was able to turn the tables on Haman. The Jews were rescued from the first potential holocaust, and Haman was impaled on his own and impaling Pole on his front lawn. How cool is that? Scripture says in Esther 4:14, "And who knows but that you have come to royal position for such a time as this?" Folks, we are just like Esther. God has divinely positioned us to save lives. That's why you live where you live. That's why you work where you work. That's why you meet every single person that you meet. Our sovereign God is constantly bringing lost people to his children and connecting them with us in various ways, hoping that we will recognize that these are divine appointments. All he wants us to do is to use that connection to invite them to go to heaven and leave the results to Him. When you get this into your head, every day becomes a great adventure! I believe that every person you meet has been handpicked by God. As we travel this planet, our sovereign God is selecting people to bring to us, hoping we'll recognize "why we are where we are," and invite them into our eternal lifeboats!

What do you think the greatest title on planet earth is? President of the United States? No. It's ambassador for Jesus Christ. When we become a follower of Jesus Christ, we get this title and all of the responsibility that goes along with it. And, folks, it is a full-time job! Yet most of us aren't even doing it part-time. It is such an important job that one day, every follower of Jesus Christ will stand before Him at a place called the Judgment Seat of Christ. There He will give us a lifetime performance review for how good of a job we did as his ambassador. In 2 Corinthians 5:20, the scripture says, "We are therefore Christ's ambassadors." Notice it doesn't say pastors are Christ's ambassadors. Missionaries are Christ's ambassadors; those who are in full-time vocational Christian service are Christ's ambassadors. It says *we*. Anyone who raises their hand and says they are a follower of Jesus Christ gets the title and all of the responsibilities that go along with it. Although our primary responsibility on planet earth is to be an ambassador for Jesus Christ, we are cleverly disguised as police officers, electricians, doctors, teachers, etc. So what is an ambassador?

An ambassador who is someone assigned by the highest authority there is to represent him in a specific place. You are assigned by the King of kings, the Lord of lords, the Creator and Sustainer of the universe to represent Him where you live, where you work, at the gas pump, at the park, on an airplane, and everywhere you go!

Did you ever notice that healthy things grow? Healthy plants grow. Healthy animals grow. Healthy people grow, and healthy churches grow. David Jeremiah said, "All living things, if they are healthy, should experience growth—and the church is no exception. Although individual churches may experience barriers to growth, those barriers should diligently be overcome. Growth is at the heart of Christ great commission."

A recent study indicated that only 1 percent of all of the evangelical churches in America grow by leading others to Christ and discipling them. That must break God's heart! It's one of the main reasons that He left us here. Another sad statistic: only 7 percent of professing followers of Jesus Christ have ever let another person to Him. Sadly, a lot of church growth in America is measured by what I'll call "sheep trading." Sheep will move from a flock on the other side of town to our church because they changed the style of music, the pastor said something that offended them, or worse yet, they painted the fellowship hall the color they didn't choose! That is *not* church growth! It is sheep trading or shuffling the deck of existing believers. Many times, when a church isn't growing numerically, the pastor gets the blame. "We hired this pastor to grow the church, and the church isn't growing, so it's his fault. Let's get rid of him and get a better one!" No! This church doesn't need a new pastor… The pastor needs a new congregation! The pastor's job is to equip the church for the work of ministry…not to do all of the work of ministry. Shepherds don't make sheep… Sheep make sheep! It's our job as the sheep of the flock to be reproducing sheep (new believers) and discipling them.

Therefore, based on your interests, your position in life, and your background, there are certain kinds of people who will listen to you, who won't listen to me, and who won't listen to your pastor. They are *your* connections. So who are some of the kinds of people who might listen to someone like you? Again, police will listen to police. Teachers will listen to teachers, medical professionals will listen to other medical professionals, tennis players will listen to other tennis players, etc. Figure out who you may be able to connect with, and look for those opportunities!

In 1 Corinthians 9:22, Paul wrote, "When I am with those who are weak, I share their weakness, for I want to bring the weak to Christ. Yes, I try to find some common ground with everyone, doing everything I can to save some." When you encounter any type of common ground, as simple as it might be, that is a divine appointment by a sovereign God.

Did you have "Show and Tell" when you were in elementary school? How did it work? Each student had to bring in something to show to the class and talk about it. This was called show and tell, and it was a two-part assignment. If you just brought something in, stood in front of the room, and said nothing, you failed the assignment. You had to talk about what you brought in. Similarly, if you want to be a successful spiritual rescuer, there is a two-part assignment. You must do both parts to get a passing grade. The first part of the assignment is to "show." What do I mean by that? I mean you need to show people that you are different because you are a follower of Jesus Christ. We need to live out our faith regardless of who the audience is. We shouldn't be Christian "chameleons."

Chuck Swindoll said, "When outsiders look at us, they should notice something different about us. We are holy because our God is holy. We are consecrated and set apart. We stand out as witnesses in the midst of an unholy an ungodly culture." Here's a statement to consider: "Biblically, if your faith hasn't changed you, then your faith hasn't saved you." The *Life Application Study Bible* comments on 2 Corinthians 5:17, "But followers of Christ are new creations, born from above and changed from within, with values and lifestyles that confront the world and clash with accepted morals. True believers don't blend in very well."

We are to be different from the lost world that we live in. God has called us to be "salt and light" in Matthew 5:13 and Acts 13:47. Salt flavors meat and preserves it. When salt and meat interact, the meat is changed forever. As salt, we are to make the world thirsty for God. Light penetrates darkness. If you take a powerful flashlight outside on a bright sunny day, you won't even know it is working. But take that light into a room with no lights and no windows, and it illuminates the whole room. Brothers and sisters, we are living in a time in history when we can see our world getting darker by the day. So that light of Christ should shine brighter as the world around us gets darker. God doesn't want what I'll call closet Christians or secret agent Christians as followers. He wants bold, unashamed followers who will let their light shine in a very dark world. And if we're *not* different from the lost world we live in, something could be terribly wrong!

David Platt said, "If you are truly a disciple of Jesus, you will be supernaturally compelled to make disciples of Jesus." Does that statement frighten you? It frightens me because I have many loved ones and friends who are professing Christians. They attend church, they are involved in the church, but what frightens me is I can't recall many of them ever telling me whom they got to share Jesus with on a given day. David Platt says that the desire to share Christ is a natural outflow when you have the Holy Spirit living inside of you. David Platt continues, "True followers of Jesus do not need to be convinced, cajoled, persuaded, or manipulated into making disciples of all nations. Everyone who follows Jesus Biblically will fish for men globally."

Regarding Matthew 5:13, the *Life Application Study Bible* says, "If Christians make no effort to affect the world around them, they are of little value to God. If we are too much like the world, we are worthless. Christians should not blend in with everyone else. Instead, we should affect others positively, just as seasoning brings out the best flavor in food."

The second part of the assignment is to "tell." We need to tell people why we are different. There are many Christians who are very good at the "show" part. But they never get around to the "tell" part. People are not going to figure it out on their own. They are not going to say, "That Don Sunshine is a really nice guy. I bet Jesus died on the cross for my sins." Those two things will not be put together unless you put them together. See, if the world believes in a God, they know that they have done things that are wrong, because God has written His Word on our hearts. They know they have lied, stolen, lusted, and used God's name in vain. So if they do believe in God, they believe they have to do something to make up for the wrongs they have done. They may choose to give money, help people, or volunteer for various organizations. They are trying to build a bridge across the huge chasm that's been created by their sin that has separated them from a perfect and holy God. We need to explain to them that the bridge is out. They can't get there the way they are going. Jesus said, "I am the way the truth and the life. No one comes to the Father but through me." Is that narrow-minded, politically incorrect, and unpopular? You bet it is, and it is only going to get worse as time goes by. Proverbs 24:11 says, "Rescue those being led away to death; hold back those staggering toward slaughter." Jude 1:23 admonishes us to "Snatch others from the fire and save them."

Penn Jillette, of Penn and Teller fame, is an atheist. He doesn't believe in God, and he made this statement: "How much do you have to hate someone, that if you believe there's a heaven and hell, and people could be going to hell, that you wouldn't tell them how to avoid it."

Wow! That stung...and from the mouth of an atheist no less! You catch watch his whole statement on YouTube by searching for "Penn gets a Bible."

David Platt said, "It is the epitome of hate to not sacrifice your very life to spread this good news among every person you know and every people group on the planet."

In summary, you are *where* you are because you have divinely positioned by a sovereign God to change lives.

A Real-Life Illustration

I have been going to Daytona Bike Week for the past twenty-one years to share the Gospel with people who have similar interests as me—motorcycles. One thing I learned about Florida is they have some of the longest traffic lights on planet earth! If you catch one of these lights, you often wonder, is it ever going to change? Is it broken? I think it would be safe to put your car in park, go have some lunch, and come back with some reading material. The light most likely will still be red. So we caught one of these red lights on our motorcycles. I was in the left part of the right lane. My friend Ron was next to me next to the shoulder, and my friend Jim was directly behind me. I looked in my mirrors to be sure I wasn't going to be rear-ended by someone not paying attention, and when I saw that it was safe, I put the motorcycle in neutral and started to relax because I knew I was going to be there for a while. I looked at the vehicle in front of me. It was a Ford Explorer, and its gas cap was hanging out, although they closed the door without screwing the cap in. So I thought for a second, put the motorcycle in first gear, pulled to the left, and drove down the dotted line to the driver's door of the Explorer. I rapped on the lady's window. She jumped, as I had startled her, rolled her window down, and said, "Can I help you?" I said, "Ma'am, do you realize that your gas cap is hanging out?" She turned to her left and looked back toward the gas cap and said, "No. I just filled it up. Didn't I screw the cap in?" I replied, "No. You just closed the door. For safety reasons and because I thought you'd like to keep what you just paid for, you really need to have that screwed in. I'm already out here. If it's okay with you, I can screw it in for you." She said, "That would be great!" I backed the motorcycle up, opened the door, screwed the cap in, and closed the door. I pulled forward to the driver's window, and she said, "Thank you so much!" I replied, "No problem. Hey, do you want to go to heaven when you die?" She said, "Yes!" I asked, "Do you know how to get to heaven?" She said, "No." I said, "Let me tell you how to get to heaven." I reached in my cargo pocket of my pants and pulled out a Gospel of John with a motorcycle-themed cover. The first thing you read is the plan of salvation in the book. In jest, I said to her, "You may be able to read through this whole book before the light turns green. But if you can't, will you take it home and read it?" She said she would and thanked me. I backed the motorcycle up, and Ron was laying on his gas tank laughing. He said he had seen me sharing the Gospel with the lady and wanted to know how I started the conversation. I told him that she had left he gas cap off. He said, "Wait a minute. What are the chances that this lady is going to leave her gas cap off? That God would put you in the only place in traffic that you could see that? Because I couldn't see it, and I asked Jim what you were doing, and he couldn't see it. And no offense, Don, that you'd be smart enough to use that situation as an open door to share your faith with this woman?" I said, "Ron, stuff like this happens to me almost every day." He said, "You see things that I don't see." I said, "Ron, I've been doing this as a lifestyle for a number of years. I just taught you this last month. Keep your eyes open and you'll start seeing things like this too."

CHAPTER 2

Every Day Ask Jesus to Break
Your Heart for the Lost

Point 1 was to recognize why *you are* where *you are.*

2.   Every day ask Jesus to break your heart for the lost.

This is part of a daily quiet time with God. You can't have a deep relationship with anyone if you don't spend time with them communicating. It must be two-way communication. The same thing is true with our Father in heaven. We need to speak to Him. That is called prayer. Satan tries to limit your praying because he knows you're praying will limit him. When we pray, we should ask Jesus to break our hearts for the lost people in our lives.

God also wants to speak with us. The way He does this is when we open His Word, read it, and apply the truths to our lives. This quiet time with God must be a priority. I believe the devil uses the busyness of life in our country to keep us from the most important things we need to do, which is deepening our relationship with our Father in heaven. If a loved one is in the hospital and you get a phone call from the local ER, I don't believe that you will look at your calendar, see how busy it is, and then tell the nurse that you couldn't get there for three days. No! You are going to push aside everything that's less important for something truly important. We need to carve out time each day to spend time with our Father in heaven. Daily application of God's Word has a purifying effect on our minds and our hearts. When we read scripture, it will point out sin. Why is that important? If you have unconfessed sin, there is no point in praying to God because He won't hear your prayers. It amazes me that some Christians wait until the first Sunday of the month when the Lord's Supper is being observed to make things right with God. We need to keep our confessions current.

It will motivate us to confess that sin and restore that relationship with our Father.

It will renew our relationship with God, which was interrupted by choosing to sin against Him.

Lastly, it will guide us back onto the right path.

It says in 1 John 1:12, "He who has the Son has life; he who does not have the Son of God does not have life." You see, either we are a follower of Jesus Christ, or we are a follower of Satan. There are no other choices. The *Life Application Study Bible* says, "It is impossible to be neutral. Every person has a master—either God or sin... You are free to choose between the two masters, but you are not free to adjust the consequences of your choice."

When you see these people as Jesus sees them, you will see them as future inhabitants of hell. The keyword here is *inhabitant*. It means they *live* there. Christians always talk about eternal life in the positive. But the truth is, everyone gets eternal life. The only question is, where are you going to spend it? Some people are going to spend eternity in a place that's beyond their wildest imaginations, wonderful. Others are going to spend it in a place that's beyond their worst nightmares, horrible. Jesus actually talked more about hell than he did about heaven. Jonathan Edwards, probably the greatest American theologian, described hell vividly, "Consider the torment of burning like a livid coal not for an instant or a day, but for millions upon millions of ages, at the end of which they would know that their torment was no nearer to an end than ever before and that they would never, never be delivered." Does that statement scare you? It does me! You see, Jesus taught that there is an ever-agonizing never-ending wrath awaiting lost sinners before a Holy God. Jesus has a command for us to make disciples of all nations, and it begins with us telling someone about him. That's why we're still on this planet.

Then the question comes up, "Do we fear God?" Fear of the Lord is a theme in the Bible from Genesis through Revelation. We are told in Scripture that fear of the Lord is the beginning of wisdom. Paul understood this! In 2 Corinthians 5:10–11, Paul said this, "For we must all appear before the judgment seat of Christ, that each one may receive what is due him for the things done while in the body, whether good or bad. Since we know what it is to fear the Lord, we try to persuade men" (or to climb into the lifeboat with us).

You see, every person's name is on one of two eternal lists in heaven. Our names are either on the eternal *lost* list or the eternal *saved* list.

A number of years ago, Cathy and I took our two oldest grandchildren to the Titanic Traveling Museum, which was in Harrisburg, Pennsylvania. When we paid for your tickets, we were given a replica of a boarding pass of a real person was on that ship that day. Each of us took on the identity of a person for the entire time that we were in the exhibit. I took on the identity of a thirty-year-old engineer named William Arthur Lobb, from Scranton, Pennsylvania, and my family members each got one as well.

I carried Mr. Lobb's boarding pass through the exhibit, and I wondered about this man. He was an American. So why was he in England? Was he there for family, vacation, or work? My daughter-in-law is from the Scranton, Pennsylvania, area. I wonder how far apart they would have lived if they lived at the same time? But the nagging question was, "Did he make it, or didn't he?" We got to find out at the end of the exhibit. There was a large white wall with an exit door in the middle of it. On the wall, on one side of the door, was a long list of names, just like in heaven. The wall on the other side of the door had a short list of names, just like in heaven. At the top of the long list, they put the word "LOST." At the top of the short list, they put the word "SAVED." We quickly compared our names to the lists, and William Arthur Lobb was the only one of the four of us on the lost list. When my ten-year-old granddaughter figured out what had happened, she looked at me and blurted out, "Poppop, you're dead!" I shrugged my shoulders and said, "Yeah." She replied, "Not us, we're all saved!" Now I would love to move Mr. Lobb from the Titanic lost list to the saved list, but I can't. He's there forever! However, it is our jobs, as full-time ambassadors for Jesus Christ, to move as many people as we can from God's eternal lost list to His eternal saved list. That's what we're equipping you to do!

CHAPTER 3

Conquer the Fears
that Stop You

Review:

Point 1 was to recognize why you are where you are.
Point 2 was to ask Jesus every day to break your heart for the lost.

3. Conquer the fears that stop you.

There is only one reason that we don't actively share our faith in Christ every day. The reason is fear. So unless we identify what the fears are and I show you how to beat those fears, you're never going to do this. The good news is I know that I can help! Let's start by listing some of the fears that keep us from sharing our faith in Christ:

Rejection. What if they reject me and/or my message? What if they ask me a question and I don't know the answer? I'll look stupid! This is one of my favorites. When are you going to have all the answers? Never! So don't worry about it! I have an associate degree in management. I don't know everything. When someone asks me a spiritual question and I don't know the answer, do you know what I say? "I don't know, but I can find out! Let's get together next week of a glass of tea, and I'll tell you what I found out." I am going to water the seed I am planting today.

I haven't memorized enough scripture yet. When will we have memorized enough scripture? Never. So don't worry about it. You

ting one passage of scripture. As
rately, in words they can under-
do the rest.

ake jokes about me, make fun of

d?

crazy.

pit of hell. When I made a com-
th every day back in 2000, I was
en I would encounter someone and
pointment by a sovereign God, my
heart would beat like a racehorse, I'd sweat, and I'd get this really
uncomfortable feeling inside. No one taught me how to defeat these
satanic lies, and they almost stopped me from sharing every time.
However, as I was reading through scripture and I gained great comfort reading how even the great apostle Paul, who wrote two-thirds
of the New Testament, was afraid too!

Look at how afraid he was. In Acts 18:9–11, Luke wrote, "One
Night the Lord spoke to Paul in a vision and told him, 'Don't be
afraid! Speak out! Don't be silent! For I am with you, and no one will
attack or harm you, for many people in the city belong to me.' So
Paul stayed there for the next year and a half…"

In 1 Corinthians 2:3–5, Paul wrote, "I came to you in weakness
and fear, and with much trembling." Wow! He was more afraid than
I! I have been part of the "weakness and fear clubs," but I have never
trembled at the thought of doing this! But let's be real… Did Paul
have a good reason for feeling this way? Think about it…when Paul
shared his faith, he was caned three times, dragged outside the city,
stoned, and left for dead. He got thirty-nine lashes five times! I bet
when we see him in glory, we will find out that getting thirty-nine
lashes five times was a world record. Many people did not survive
one round of thirty-nine lashes, because they died tied to the tree.

They were disemboweled through their backs. What are my
fears compared to his? They might laugh at me… They might make
fun of me… They might call me names… Really? How awful does

that sound? The next part of this passage contains a tremendous promise.

"My message and my preaching were not with wise and persuasive words, but with a demonstration of the Spirit's power, so that your faith may not rest on men's wisdom, but in God's power." Wow! What a promise to claim! Let's analyze a little. If Jesus came to seek and to save the lost and I try to seek and save the lost, will it please God? Yes! So what's the promise? He'll give me the power to do that. If Jesus commanded us to make disciples and I try to make disciples, will it please God? Yes! Again, the promise is that He will give us the power to be obedient!

Here's a quote that will sting. W. E. Sangster, a British pastor of a Wesleyan Church, said this, "How shall I feel at the judgment if multitudes of missed opportunities pass before me in full review and all of my excuses proved to be disguises of my cowardice and pride?" Are we too cowardly and proud to say something? The opposite is courageous and humble. I am trying to move my life a little more in the direction each day.

To fight these fears, I think it's important to remember who's in charge. In Ezekiel 36:26–27, it is written, "I'll give you a new heart and put a new spirit in you; I will remove from you your heart of stone and give you a heart of flesh. And I will put my Spirit in you and move you to follow my decrees and be careful to keep my laws." When you trust Christ as your Lord and Savior, the Holy Spirit enters you and begins to change you. One of the byproducts of that is that you have a new desire to follow God's decrees and keep his laws. If you don't have that, you are not saved. It is impossible to have this supernatural encounter with the living God and not walk away different.

I like the way the *New Living Translation* translates Philippians 2:13. It says, "Work hard to show the results of your salvation, obeying God with deep reverence and fear. For God is working in you, giving you the desire and the power to do what pleases him." This is another great promise! What are the results of my salvation? I am going to begin obeying God with deep reverence in fear. There's that *fear* word again. God promises to give us the desire and the power to do what pleases him in this verse. If Jesus commanded us to make disciples and I try to make disciples by telling them about my faith, will it please God? Yes! So what's the promise? He'll give me the power to do that!

Where does this power come from? It comes from His indwelling Holy Spirit! Timothy 1:7–8 says, "For God has not given us a Spirit of fear and timidity, but of power, love, and self-discipline. So never be ashamed to tell others about the Lord." And in Luke 12:11–12, the scripture says, "Don't worry about how to defend yourself or what to say, for the Holy Spirit will teach you at that time what needs to be said." It's amazing to me that when we recognize the prompting of the Holy Spirit to share our faith with someone and we allow the Holy Spirit to speak through us, words start coming out of our mouths that we didn't plan on saying. And oftentimes, it isn't even our style of sharing. It doesn't negate our responsibility to study to be a workman approved. But it's amazing what happens when you let the Holy Spirit take control of a situation and conversation.

One of the best ways that I can think of to illustrate this point is to say that you are just "God's glove." What do I mean by that? If I lay a glove down on a table and command it to pick up my water bottle, will it do it? No. What if I yell and scream at the glove? Will that make a difference? No. But when I insert my hand into the glove and command it to pick up the water bottle, it does it very well. Brothers and sisters, we are just like that glove. We are powerless to do these things on our own. But when we allow the indwelling Holy Spirit to empower us, we can do anything God wants us to do.

A Real-Life Illustration

Let me illustrate with a true story. I am going to introduce you to four people. Joe and Leigh are Italian Catholics from the Finger Lakes of New York. Someone shared the Gospel with them, the Father drew them to Himself through his Holy Spirit, and they surrendered their lives to the Lordship of Christ in repentance and faith. They were born again! Now they wanted to take Leigh's parents, Tony and

Jean, to heaven with them. Joe and Leigh tried to share the Gospel with them whenever the family got together, typically at birthdays and big holidays. The sharing often descended into screaming arguments. So they stopped talking and started praying.

At the time, Cathy and I attended a small church, which met in an American Legion Hall in Prattsburgh, New York. We had a layperson, named Karmon, who was preaching every Sunday as we had no ordained pastor. One day, Karmon got a call from Joe, who told him that his father-in-law, Tony, was in the Bath Hospital suffering from kidney failure. Tony was refusing to get dialysis, and the doctor said without dialysis, Tony would die in less than two months. Joe felt he could not go and prayed for Tony because he knew it would just start another heated argument. So he told Karmon, that because he was the "pastor" of the church, he wanted Karmon to go to the hospital to pray for Tony and share the Gospel with him. Karmon said he would go, but he asked Joe if he would mind if he took Don (me) with him because Don was raised Catholic and Don knew what Catholics believed. Joe agreed. So Karmon asked me to go along with him. As I was driving to the hospital with Karmon sitting next to me, there was some serious spiritual warfare going on. I wasn't teaching this material yet, so I didn't understand the battle that was occurring in the unseen world. The demons were working Karmon over, throwing every fear that they could into his mind.

He asked me if he could confess something to me. I said, "Sure." He told me that he was the pastor because there was no one else to preach. All he had was a high school education, he had never been to the hospital to pray for anyone, and he was scared to death to do this.

Karmon reminded me of all of the testimonies he had heard me share and asked me if I would take the lead on this because didn't know what to do or say. I told him that I would take the lead on this, but I had never been to the hospital to pray with anyone either. As we parked the car in the parking lot, I suggested to Karmon that we pray. We prayed for Tony, the Lord's guidance, and that He would accomplish whatever it was He wanted to accomplish by us being there. We entered the hospital and went down the hallway of the intensive care wing. There stood Joe outside of Tony's door with the door closed.

He thanked us both for coming and said that he had taken time off work to meet us at the hospital. He told us that he needed to tell us something about Tony before we went in to see him. Joe told us that Tony was so against what we believed that when we tried to share our faith with him, he might get up out of his bed, grab us by the scruff of her neck and the seat of our pants, and physically throw us out of his room! Then he added, "Please, please understand. I am not exaggerating one bit!" I was stunned! I looked at Karmon and said, "Karmon, did you know this was going to happen? Is that why you stuck this on me on the way over here?" Karmon assured me that he had no idea this was going to happen.

I asked Joe how old Tony was. He said, "Eighty-four." I knew I could take on an eighty-four-year-old and come out the victor, but I didn't sign up for this! I certainly didn't know that I might be involved in hand-to-hand combat with this older man, so I suggested the three of us hold hands and pray for the situation before we entered the room. As we entered the room, Tony was sitting on the edge of the bed eating something. I introduced myself and Karmon to him and told him that we went to church with his daughter Leigh. He said, "That's nice." I asked him if anyone had been in to see him and pray for him, and he said, "No." I told him that we had come to the hospital to pray for him and asked him if that would be okay. He replied, "Yes." Then I asked him an important question…remember this question… I asked him what he believed.

He told me that he was a Catholic. I replied, "So was I. Let me tell you my story." I sat down and shared my personal hope story or testimony with him. At the end of the story, I told Tony that he had just heard God's plan of salvation for every human being. Would he like to make a decision right now to surrender whatever time he has left on planet earth to the Lordship of Jesus Christ, turn from his sins, place his faith and trust in Jesus Christ to save him, and commit to follow him for the rest of his life? I explained to him that if he made this decision right now, and kidney failure killed him two hours from now, he would go straight to heaven. Tony said, "It sounds good, but I don't want to do it." I said, "That's okay. Can we pray for you now?" He agreed. I explained to him that many times in the Bible they would lay hands on people when they prayed for them. Would it be okay if we put our hands on his shoulder when we prayed for him? Tony agreed. Karmon and I placed our hands on his shoulders, and I prayed for his healing and his salvation. Tony thanked me and asked if I had a business card. I gave him my business card, and he said that he would be out of the hospital in a couple of days and might invite us up for coffee. Sounds good! Karmon and I left the room and closed the door, and I said, "Karmon, this couldn't have gone much better! We were a hundred percent successful!" Karmon asked how I came to that conclusion. I told him that my only goal in coming to the hospital that day was to plant the Gospel seed in Tony's heart. Now it's up to God to cause the growth. He didn't try to throw us out, so we didn't have to wrestle him to the floor in a wrist lock; he might invite us up to his home for coffee, and the only way it could have gone better is if he had given his life to our Lord right then. We left the hospital, and a few days later, Karmon called me at Family Life and told me that he had just received a phone call from Joe. The doctors in Bath were baffled because after we left, Tony's kidney failure mysteriously disappeared, and they had no explanation of what had happened! Praise God! He healed Tony!

About four months went by, and I was walking to the kitchen table before church with a bowl of cereal in my hands, and the Holy Spirit prompted me to do something. Now I was a Christian for a lot of years and never understood when the Holy Spirit was prompting me do something. So I reasoned that if I didn't know when this was happening, probably a lot of other followers of Christ didn't know as well. How do you know the Holy Spirit is prompting you to do something? Does the room you're in shake, pictures start falling off the wall, and Charlton Heston's voice come thundering through your home? Of course not! Let me suggest the following:

A thought comes to mind—often out of nowhere. Now it's not just any random thought… When Cathy and a have a long drive to get to a church to minister, we usually will have a nice breakfast at home, skip lunch to save time and money, stop for fuel and bathroom breaks, arrive at our destination around dinnertime, and have a nice dinner before setting up at the church. When we have this type of a travel schedule, I can almost guarantee that about 2:30 p.m., a thought will enter my mind. Do you know what it is? Chick-fil-A! "Cathy, the Holy Spirit just told me we need to stop at the next Chick-fil-A!" No…that was my stomach sending the thought to my brain. So how do you know when it's the Holy Spirit? When the thought says to

Do something good for someone. Get a clue… That thought didn't come from you. Be obedient, and do what you were prompted to do. Maybe it's help your neighbor do something, or put $200 cash in an envelope and mail it to them because they need it now. Whatever it is, do it now.

Pray for *someone.* Have you ever been in a situation when you're not thinking specifically about anything and the name of a person pops into your head? Perhaps the Lord is bringing them to your mind because they need prayer right then. Stop what you're doing and pray for them.

A Real-Life Illustration

I have a friend named John, who travels to India every year on a missions trip. One year he was going there, and his wife was coming along with him. He told me their schedule, and I told him that I would be praying for them they were away. On Thursday of the week they were away, I was walking into my garage, and John popped in my head. I stopped what I was doing and said, "God, I don't know why you laid John in my heart right now, but let me pray for him." I prayed for them and went about my business. After they returned from their trip, he was filling me in on what the Lord had done in India, and I asked him if anything out of the ordinary had happened on Thursday? He asked me what time, and I gave him a rough time period. He did the time zone calculations in his head and told me that while I was praying for them, they were casting demons out of a woman outside of a brothel! Wow!

Pray with *someone.* This is awkward the first few times you do this. Trust me, the demons will be working your fear buttons over because they don't want you praying for anyone. It does get easier as you do it more often. More about this later…

Share Jesus with them. If you feel this prompting, tell them about your faith in Christ and how He saved you and changed your life.

It doesn't go away. The "Hound of Heaven," the Holy Spirit, will keep bringing this to mind until you're obedient and do it.

Here's what popped into my head that morning, "Go see Tony and Jean." I knew right away that this was the Holy Spirit as I wasn't thinking about Tony or Jean at that point in time. I went to church and found Leigh. I asked her where her parents lived. She asked me why I was asking that question. I told her that the Holy Spirit had prompted me that morning to go and see them. She said, "Oh, good! Since my dad was healed and came home from the hospital, Mom suffered a slight stroke. It isn't very serious, but she isn't allowed to drive until the slight disability is corrected. My dad can't drive anymore, because his eyes aren't good enough. So they are stuck all day in this double-wide trailer fighting like cats and dogs! It's really ugly!" I thought, "Wonderful! Sounds like a fun visit!" She asked me when I would go to see them, and I told her that I couldn't do it tomorrow but I would do it on Tuesday.

Tuesday, I was sitting in my office at around noontime, totally forgetting that I was supposed to go see Tony and Jean, and the Holy Spirit again prompted me to go. I recognized it, told the Lord I was sorry for forgetting, and headed to their home. As I was driving the roughly ten miles to their home, I was praying. Also, something bad was happening. Can you guess what it was? My fear buttons were being pushed fast and furiously. Here's what was popping into my head: "Who do you think you are? You're not a pastor! You don't have any counseling training! You are a youth action director. Your gifts lie with teenagers. These people are senior citizens in their eighties! You can't relate to them, you have nothing in common with them, and you have nothing to share with them! You have more important things to do at the ministry. Turn the car around and go back."

I had knots in my stomach, but I continued to drive. When I parked in their driveway, I sat in the car for a few minutes and prayed. Then I got out and walked up to the front door. Before I rang the doorbell, I raised my hands and prayed, "God, I am here because you told me to be here. You know my heart. You know that I am scared to death to do this, and I don't know what to say or even how to start the conversation. But I surrender to you and pray that your Holy Spirit will speak through me. I pray that You will accomplish whatever it is that You want to accomplish by me being here and that You will receive honor and glory for whatever happens…in Jesus's name."

I rang the doorbell, and Tony came to answer the door. The meeting didn't start out really well! He screamed at me, "What do you want!" I said, "Tony, I'm Don. Do you remember me?" He screamed, "No. I don't remember you. What do you want?" I said, "I'm the guy who prayed for you while you were in the hospital with kidney failure." He paused, thought for a second, and said, "I remember you! I'm sorry, come in." I walked in, and he introduced me to his wife, Jean. He motioned for me to sit on the central chair in the living room. I'll call it the Archie Bunker chair, and I sat down. My weight began to compress seat cushion. My arms started out at normal height at my side but quickly we're being raised up to almost shoulder level as I sank deeper into the chair. That seat cushion was totally worn out! The cushion had totally collapsed, and as my butt hit the wooden base of the chair, about five to six wasps flew out of the chair and started buzzing around my head! I started swatting them away, and Tony and Jean just sat there looking at me. Tony finally said, "Don't worry about them, Don. Our cats will get them sooner or later!" I asked if their cats still had their claws because I thought this could get really ugly if they launched themselves at the wasps buzzing around my head! More distractions… I asked Tony if he had given any more thought to what I shared with him in the hospital. He said, "Nope, not for a minute!" Isn't this going great? I said, "Jean, you weren't in the hospital when I shared with Tony." Let me tell you what I said. As

I started to talk, something happened that I had never experienced before. (Insert hand in the glove). Words started coming out of my mouth that I wasn't thinking of saying! And what made it even more bizarre was that it wasn't my style! I jumped right in their faces and started challenging them for not listening to their daughter's loving attempts to take them to heaven with her. Tony threw out an objection at one point, and I used an illustration of a turnstile in the subways of New York that I have never used before. I thought, "That was really good! I'll have to remember that illustration for some future occasion." After about an hour and thirty minutes, two people in their eighties told me that they wanted to go to heaven! I was blessed to lead them to faith in Christ in their living room. I prayed for each of them and said, "In Jesus's name, amen," and walked over to Jean. I asked her to stand up so I could be the first one to welcome her to the family of God with a huge hug. She stood up, and I hugged her. I told her that the Bible says there is great rejoicing in the presence of angels in heaven over her decision to repent and trust Christ and that God was preparing an eternal home for her. I turned and walked over to Tony. He looked up at me and shook his head from side to side as if to say, "You're not hugging me!" I said, "Be a man and stand up! I'm going to hug you too!" Tony stood up, and I gave him a big hug as well. I asked each of them if they made this decision with their whole heart. They both said they had. I told him that in Romans 10:9–10, God says that they need to confess with their mouth what they have done. I asked if they were willing to tell someone that they just gave their life to Jesus Christ. Tony said, "Absolutely! Who do you think we should tell?" I suggested they tell their daughter Leigh because it would make her day. Tony said she wouldn't be home until later that night but that they would call and tell her of their decision.

I thanked them for letting me come and talk to them that day and left. As I began the drive back to the ministry, the magnitude of what happened started to hit me. I knew I didn't do this! It was all the Holy Spirit! I started shaking so badly that I thought if I didn't pull off to the side of the road I was going to wreck the car and probably kill myself. When I stopped the car and parked on the side of the road, I burst into tears and cried for probably two minutes! I kept asking God, "What just happened back there? Did I imagine this?" It was surreal! It impacted me so greatly that I had to stop the car three separate times during the ten-mile ride back to the ministry because I couldn't safely operate the vehicle. When I got back to the ministry, I shared with everyone what the Holy Spirit had done. Everyone was praising God because Joe was on the board of directors of Family Life, and they cared deeply for him.

Cathy and I had to go shopping after work, and on the way home from the store, I told her that I hoped that Joe had called me while we were out because that meant that Tony had called them to tell them of their decision to follow Christ. After arriving at home, I was bringing the groceries up the steps to the kitchen, and Cathy was checking the voice mail on our home phone. As I brought the last batch of groceries upstairs, she handed me a note and told me that Joe had called and asked me to call him back. I called Joe and said, "Joe, it's Don Sunshine. I'm returning your call." Joe said, "Don, how do we thank you?" I told Joe that he didn't have to thank me. I was just being obedient to what the Holy Spirit was telling me to do, and God gets all the honor and glory. Joe said that they had been trying to reach her parents for years and they would never listen. He wanted to know what I said to convince them to follow Christ. I told him I didn't know! I only remembered bits and pieces of what I said. The Holy Spirit was doing all of the speaking. I asked where Leigh was, and he told me she was unconscious on the couch! I jokingly said, "Go check her and make sure she's breathing!" He laughed and said she's alive. I asked what happened. Joe said that Tony called and Leigh answered the phone. Tony said, "Leigh, it's your dad. Your friend Don was here today, and your mom and I turned from our sins and trusted Christ as our Savior. Here, talk to your mother." How great is that! Jean took the phone and said, "Leigh, we are so excited! Your dad and I are going to heaven with you and the kids!" Praise the Lord!

Tony took the phone from his wife and said, "Leigh, I can't explain this, but ever since your friend Don was here today, I feel like I need to read the Bible. I've never read the Bible a day in my life! What do I do? My eyes aren't good enough to read anymore!" Leigh told her dad that they have the Bible on tape and that she would buy it for him. Tony listened to the Bible tapes every day for the rest of his life. When he went home to be with the Lord about eighteen months later, I went to the funeral home to meet Leigh. I met her in the lobby and gave her a big hug. I told her how sorry I was for her loss but I was rejoicing that her dad was home in heaven. She told me that she wanted me to go say hello to her mom. I asked if her mom would remember me. Lee said, "My mom will never forget you!" She led me into a room, and at the far end of the room was her mom sitting in a big stuffed chair. When she saw me, she smiled and motioned for me to come over to her. When I got close, she asked me to kneel down beside her chair. I knelt down on both knees beside her chair. She took both of my hands inside of hers and thanked me three times for coming to share Jesus with them that day. She told me she was at peace, knowing where Tony was, and someday she would be going there as well. She also mentioned that she'd see Joe and Leigh, the kids, and me there! I smiled and agreed. I told her that she didn't have to thank me for sharing with them that day. It was one of the most memorable experiences I had ever had as a believer, and I prayed that God would give fifty or one hundred more of these in my lifetime.

Brothers and sisters, when you experience something like this, it changes your life forever! And the good news is that not one of you can dismiss this and say God can't do that through you. Yes, He can, and He wants to! But we must be surrendered, listening to His prompting, and then be obedient. God will do the rest!

David Jeremiah said, "In order for us to be sensitive to the Spirit's leading, we must spend time getting to know His voice, because the more intimately we know Him, the easier it will be to hear His voice above all the others." I was reading through the *Life Application Study Bible*, and I saw the perfect illustration of what happened to me at Tony and Jean's. It says, "God always gives us the strength to do what He has commanded. The strength may not be evident, however, until we step out in faith and actually begin doing the task." If I elected to blow off the Holy Spirit's prompting and stay in my office that afternoon, was there any reason for God to give me the strength to go and talk with them? No. But when I went, in spite of the fear, He took control of the whole meeting, and He gets all the honor and glory and praise. I am just grateful to have been a small part in His plan.

Hopefully, this true story will inspire you to start being obedient, because God can use you as well. So the question is, how do I start? Let me illustrate with a couple of true stories. When I was a senior in high school, I was sick for a week. When I returned to school, I went to my English class. I selected a seat in about the second or third row in the middle of the room. About thirty other students filled in the other chairs. The teacher came in, clapped her hands, and announced, "It's group presentation day. We have to get all five presentations done this class period. So let's break up into our groups and get started." Every student in the room stood up and began moving their chairs around the perimeter of the classroom. I sat there stunned, looking around, trying to figure out what I was supposed to do. I had no idea what was happening in class that day. Part of me said, go sit with your buddies on the football team because you can be part of their group. But that was even more weird because I had no idea what they were going to do or say. I wasn't part of any group. As uncomfortable as it was, I sat in the middle of the room, and I was the audience for the day because I was totally unprepared for what was happening in class. Contrast that, with when I left the police department. I was twenty-seven years old and attending a county college learning about computer programming. I was in a systems analysis class, and the instructor announced on the first day of class that there was going to be some good news and some bad news. She started with the bad news. She said, "Everyone in this class is going to have to do an oral report this semester, and it will count as half of your grade." Everyone collectively moaned. She continued, "The good news is you can choose any topic you want as long as it's related to computers. Who would like to go first?" For the first time in my life, I instantly raise my hand and volunteered to go first. I was working at a little computer store selling Apple IIs with 48K of RAM, a single floppy disk drive, and an RF modulator to connect to your TV set for $1,840. I knew something about computers! I brought in an Apple II, popped the cover, and showed and explained the RAM and the ROM chips and expansion slots. I was done and got an A. The professor asked who wanted to go next, and the young fellow next to me held a book up in front of his face so he wouldn't be called upon. I encouraged him to go next, and he told me he was scared to death to do this. I suggested he do it now and get it over with so he could relax for the rest of the semester. He didn't take my advice. In fact, he had a plan for every class period so he wouldn't be called on. I don't remember everything he did, but I do remember what he did in one class. When she asked for a volunteer, he dropped his pen on the floor, kicked it across the room, and began crawling on the floor to retrieve his pen. I was stunned! I told him I would be surprised if he didn't have ulcers by the end of the semester.

What's the difference in these two scenarios? In the first story, I was totally unprepared, so I was very uncomfortable. In the second situation, I was 100 percent prepared, so I was confident. My admonition to you is to "be prepared."

If I were to gauge my level of fear when I began doing this, it was probably close to 100 percent. No one taught me how to overcome these fears. I knew I needed to be obedient to Christ and share my faith, but I also knew that I had to figure out how to defeat these fears that were stopping me. What I experienced was when I began carrying a good, accurate, written gospel tool to share with the people God connected me with, about 80 percent of my fear went away. Another 10 percent went away when I expected the person I was sharing with to say, "No. I don't want to give my life to Jesus Christ." That left me with about 10 percent of the total fear to deal with. Everyone can defeat a 10 percent fear level.

I surveyed the first ten thousand people that I trained. I would ask the question, "How many of you were saved the very first time you heard the Gospel message?" Only seven hands went up in the first ten thousand people. I realized that the salvation decision is a process. Point A is where they hear the gospel, and point B is where they make a decision to follow Christ. I've read statistics that suggest that it takes the average person between seven and twenty-five times of hearing the Gospel message and understanding it and then to be willing to make the decision to surrender, repent, place their faith and trust in Christ, and commit to follow Him. You don't know where you are in that process. You just want to be a faithful link in that process.

When you understand this, it is very easy to permanently disable the "rejection button." If you expect the person to say, "No, I don't want to do this," you are never disappointed when they don't want to trust Christ right then, and the rejection button never works again! Their response to your offer to trust Christ as their Savior is irrelevant. Again, all God wants you to do is to tell them they're in trouble and how to get out of the trouble… Plant and water seeds and then leave the results to God. You can disable the rejection right now by not worrying what their response will be to your offer. You then work on disabling the other fear buttons over time as your grow into this and put it into practice.

Here's some good news for you: did you ever notice that it is easier to share the Gospel with people you *don't know* than people you *do know*? Mark Cahill, in his book *The Watchman*, did a survey of all four Gospels in the book of Acts. He found that more than four out of five of the witnessing encounters in Scripture occurred between total strangers. This is great news! And I believe that this statistic applies today as well. We have a small finite group of people whom we know and see every day. Then there's this vast sea of lost and dying people out there. There are many more people in the sea than in the small finite group of people that we know. Every day our sovereign God is handpicking people out of this vast sea and bringing them to us in divine appointments. His hope is that we will recognize these divine appointments, share the Gospel with these people, and leave the results to Him.

For this group of people you don't know, I am going to strongly suggest that you *always* be prepared with some of these Gospels of John with the plan of salvation in the front or some good *accurate* biblical tracts. I want to emphasize two words here. Always means always. You don't know when you were going to have a divine appointment. Almost exclusively, I wear what are called operator pants, which are kind of like police SWAT pants. They have tons of pockets, and each leg has a large cargo pocket on it. I have a leather pouch that I had made up that contains an assortment of Gospel literature that I can select from when God connects me with someone. I keep that pouch in my left thigh pocket. I also have Gospel literature in my truck, in my wife's car, in my motorcycle saddlebag, and also in my home because God connects with people in all of these places and I want to be prepared.

The second word I want to emphasize is the word *accurate*. Here's the problem: over the years in the United States, we have watered down the Gospel to the point where a lot of Gospel literature does not give an accurate presentation of what we need to do to be saved. No one has evil intentions, but if you examine some of this literature in comparison to Scripture, you're going to see very little in common. The easiest way to determine an accurate Gospel tract from an inaccurate one is the tract needs to mention *repentance* in word or description. If repentance isn't mentioned in word or description, do not buy it, and do not give it to anyone! For all you will do is create a false convert. So you need to read the Gospel literature that you will be using before you give it to someone. Here are some of the Gospel literature sources that are biblically accurate, and I like to use the following:

- www.majestic-media.com: The Bridge Tract—this is a very simple way of clearly explaining the Gospel to someone with words and pictures. For twenty dollars, you can purchase a hundred of these Gospel tracts. Trust me, it will take a long time to share a hundred of these. I like to use these in our church's food  pantry as I sit among the people waiting to pick up their food. I'll have a spiritual conversation with them and take them through the Bridge Tract so they can simply understand what it means to be saved. I have been blessed to lead people to Christ in the food pantry using this tract.

- www.billygrahambookstore.org: Steps to Peace with God— this very colorful, graphic tract uses the bridge illustration to present the Gospel. It's a little fancier than the bridge tract. The pricing for this tool is the same as the bridge tract.

- www.livingwaters.com: Ray Comfort's Way of the Master Fulfillment House—there are a variety of very good, accurate Gospel tracks at this site. I purchased their sample pack because I couldn't decide what I wanted, as the selection is very large. I opened the sample pack, laid all of the Gospel literature out of my dining room table, and selected about three or four that I thought would fit my style of sharing. I purchased them and used them up.

- www.markcahill.org: *One Second After You... Die*—Mark is an author. He has written a number of books about sharing your faith. This little booklet is a summary of one of his books. I carry at least one of these with me for when I encounter an atheist or agnostic. This little booklet does a tremendous apologetics presentation, proving that the Bible is a supernatural book, the Word of God, before it gives an accurate Gospel presentation, including the need to repent. Has another booklet called *The Second Greatest Lie Ever Told*. This booklet goes through many of the religions that we find in the United States, what is wrong with them, and how Christianity is the only way to have a relationship with our Creator.

- www.ptl.org: The Pocket Testament League—this one-hundred-plus-year-old organization offers Gospels of John with the plan of salvation presented in the front of each of the Gospels. It is free to join and for twenty dollars, you can get thirty Gospels of John. Again, it will take you some time to share all thirty that you get with your order. When you join, if you don't have the money, you can even apply for a scholarship, and they will send you your order free of charge. Oh, by the way, *there are never any shipping charges.* They have over four hundred different-themed covers in several languages. You select covers based on the type of people you   believe you're going to connect with, and you can mix and match cover designs in one order. For example, when I travel to Daytona for Daytona Bike Week, I don't fill my saddlebag with Gospels of John with a pretty rose-themed cover and the title that says *A Story of Perfect Love.* If you hand that to some biker dude, you may get punched in the nose, or it will get thrown out in the first trash can that he can find. However, that same biker dude will gladly accept a Gospel of John with motorcycle handlebars on the cover and the title that says *The Perfect Road.* You carry an assortment of covers with you based on the type of person you think you're going to connect with. If you want to join the league, you can join online. They will ask you for a referral ID. *Please use my referral ID number: 124064.* One of the best parts  of using this particular tool is that when you join, you are given a membership number. When your Gospel order arrives at your home, there will be a strip of stickers with your membership number printed on them included as well. There is a place in the back of the Gospel to place your membership sticker. Why do that? This is the only written Gospel literature that I know of that can actually provide you with feedback as to what happens when you share this with someone. When a person contacts the league with a testimony or when they get saved, you get an e-mail with what happened! How cool is that? Here is one of the letters I received from the league.

THE POCKET TESTAMENT LEAGUE   Sign In | Order | Donate | Sponsor

A Gospel you shared has changed a life!

Dear Mr. Sunshine:

Dana H. of Honeybrook, PA has filled out our decision page, indicating a decision for Christ! Your referral ID was shown as the source of that Gospel of John.

Thank you for sharing!

Your faithful sharing of the gospel of John is making a difference. Thank you! As Scripture tells us, "so is my word that goes out from my mouth: It will not return to me empty, but will accomplish what I desire and achieve the purpose for which I sent it." Keep up the good work.

View your impact

To review the members you have impacted through your sharing efforts, just sign in to the web site. In your profile home page you'll see a summary of information showing your involvement in spreading the Gospel message. A left-side navigation menu gives you additional viewing options, such as your **member referral report** and even **maps** showing where people you've sponsored, referred, or who have responded, are located.

Your username is: flmmad. Your password is not shown in this message for security reasons.

In Christ,

Mike Brickley
President

Let's assume that you're prepared. You've ordered some type of Gospel literature to share with people that will, from my experience, eliminate about 80 percent of the fear. When God connects you with a lost person through a divine appointment, how do you turn the conversation from whatever it is that connected you to what God wants you to talk about? I can comfortably guarantee that if you've been a follower of Jesus Christ for any amount of time, there have been times when you felt the prompting of the Holy Spirit to tell someone about your faith, but you couldn't make the transition in the conversation. So the encounter ends, the lost person walks away, and you feel guilty because you didn't say anything God wanted you to say. Are you with me? We've all experienced this. I am going to give you six questions that you can use to turn any conversation from whatever it is you're talking about do what God wants you to talk about.

The first transitional question or conversation turner was the same question I asked Tony in the hospital. It is this: *What do you believe?* I used this question on my chiropractor, the man I bought my truck from, the man I bought my trailer from, and a sixteen-year-old teen from Utah. None was offended by this question.

Has anyone given you one of these yet? You will extend your hand and offer them the piece of Gospel literature that you have chosen for them.

Can I share something with you? I use this one a lot. As I ask this question, I am already reaching for the piece of Gospel literature that I have chosen to give them. This next part is *very* important. I have literally done this tens of thousands of times, and I have *never* had someone say, "No. You can't share something with me." Whenever you connect with someone, even at the simplest of levels, they *always* say, "Yes." Remember that. Now at a minimum, if this is a short encounter, I will say something like this after they agree to let me share with them, "You know we're all going to die someday. We can't avoid it. And we're going to stand before a perfect and Holy God guilty of breaking His laws, because we've all lied. We've all stolen. We've all lusted. We've all used God's name in vain. And the problem is that God can't tolerate sin in His presence, so we will be judged and sent to hell for eternity. However, God loved us so much that He sent His Son, Jesus Christ, to earth about two thousand years ago to pay the debt that you and I owe God in full. He did this when He died on the cross in our place and was raised from the dead. This booklet or tract is going to tell you how you can be forgiven and spend eternity with God. I'd like to give this to you as a gift. Would you take it home and read it?" That's not hard! Everyone can do that! Recognize that we are in spiritual warfare for the souls of people. The devil or his demons will lie to you and say, "Don't give that to him! He's not interested." That's another lie from the pit of hell. I have done this tens of thousands of times, and I've only had five people, in total, who have refused to take the literature I offered them. So don't believe that lie when it pops into your head.

Now if you have the time, you can have a longer conversation with the person that God just connected with.

A Real-Life Illustration

I was scheduled to teach at a church in Cape May Courthouse, New Jersey. I drove up on a Friday to the old-fashioned motor lodge that Cathy had made a reservation for me at. As I entered the motor lodge, there were two women standing behind the desk. They welcomed me and asked what my name was. When I told them my last name was Sunshine, they didn't believe me! After numerous attempts, I pulled out my driver's license and proved to them that my last name was actually Sunshine. The conversation continued:

They asked me where I was from. I replied Tennessee.
They asked me if I drove all the way to New Jersey that day. I told them I had, and it took about eleven hours. They asked me why I was there. I told him I would be teaching in a church tomorrow.

They asked me what I teach. I replied lifestyle evangelism.
They asked what that is.

So I spent an hour and forty minutes standing at the front desk talking to Susan, who was an atheist born and raised in Taiwan, and Jill, who was raised Catholic but wasn't practicing any religion now. What was I going to do? Go to my room and watch TV when I had two ladies willing to listen to spiritual things? I decided to use the "Way of the Master" technique to share the Gospel with them.

When I mentioned the Ten Commandments, Susan asked, "The ten what? What are the Ten Commandments?"

Jill laughed and said, "You never heard of the Ten Commandments?"

Jill and I both rattled off several of the Commandments, and Susan replied, "Everyone knows you're not supposed to do those things!"

I asked her how she knew she wasn't supposed to do them.

She replied, "It's built in," pointing to her heart.

I asked her who built it in.

She replied, "I don't know."

I told her, "God built it in!" I then said, "Susan, what are the chances that you could walk into a library, select sixty-six different books written by forty different authors. These authors ranged from kings all the way down the social scale to shepherds. Most of these authors didn't even know each other. These books were written over a period of 1,500 years, on three different continents, in three different languages. And when you assembled the sixty-six books into one volume, there would be one central theme running through all of them, with no contradictions or errors."

Susan replied, "That's impossible!" "That's right," I replied. "Except for the Bible. It's a supernatural book. It is the Word of God!" Susan then said, "I like the way you talk. I now believe that there is a God and that this book you're talking about is a supernatural book. Can anyone come to the thing that you're doing tomorrow?" I told them yes and invited both ladies to come.

Susan showed up on time, but Jill didn't come. Susan mentioned to me that she had to leave at 10:45 a.m. to pick up her husband.

But she would return and bring him with her. I told her we have a natural break at 10:30, and that would be a great time for her to grab a snack and leave. Susan returned with her husband and sat through the whole training. When the training ended, I was swarmed with people at my table, and I saw her slip out the side door. I was disappointed because I wanted to thank her for coming and talk with her before she left. The pastor approached me and said that Susan had given him her evaluation form and apologized for having to leave in such a hurry. The pastor said Susan told him that she had just given her life to Jesus Christ! She asked what time was church and how should she dress because she's never been to a church before! Wow! That lady was an atheist the night before! I can't explain that. That was all God! What a privilege to be a part of the process. So if you have the time, have a longer conversation with people.

Or you could use one of these questions:

Do you go to church anywhere? That will give you a clue as to what they believe and how to proceed.

Do you ever think about spiritual things?

Or one of my favorites, *If you were to die suddenly, where would you spend eternity?* This one is a little bit more "in your face," but I am liking it more by the day.

These are sixth-grade questions to memorize, because this is where we all get stuck! We have to have a way to turn the conversation once we connect with someone so we can speak about what God wants us to speak to them about. I would highly recommend that you memorize all six of these. But if you're lazy, pick two! *Can I share with you? Or if you were to die suddenly today, where would you spend eternity?*

For that other group of people, the people you know and see every day, I would suggest making a list and praying for these people every day by name. Don't generalize and lump all of these people into a prayer to "save all my friends." I don't really care where you write it down; just write it down. And when you have your quiet time with God, go down the list, name by name, and ask him to save each of these people and to use you if He wants to.

Here's a tough question, "If God saved everyone you prayed for this morning, how many people would be saved?" Think about it!

Then you want to consistently show these people who know you that you're different, and look for opportunities to tell them why you're different. These are the people who know that you have been a no good dirty rotten scoundrel. But when they see a consistently changed life, they are going to know that something happened to you. Look for opportunities to tell them what happened to you. You see, a changed life convinces people that Jesus has power. And it is often the most effective way to influence someone you know. I love Paul Washer! He said, "The evidence of salvation, the evidence of repentance, the evidence of faith, is a changed and changing life." When you are born again, some things in your life change instantly. The Holy Spirit indwells you and continues to change you as you are sanctified over time. People need to see this change in our lives, and we need to explain to them what happened.

May I make a suggestion? When you have your quiet time with God every day, I'd like you to pray a simple prayer called the Three Open Prayer. Ron Hutchcraft was reading through the book of Colossians, and he created this amazing little prayer that has three "Opens" in it. It's not a magical, mystical prayer, but I believe there are some things are true about it.

First, if you're praying the prayer from your heart, you'll be sensitive to the opportunities that God will give you to share Christ with someone that day.

Second, if you ask God to bring you people to share with, trust me, He's going to answer that in a hurry!

So where does that prayer come from? Colossians 4:3-4 says, "And pray for us, too, that God may open a door for our message, so that we may proclaim the mystery of Christ, for which I am in chains… Pray that I may proclaim it clearly as I should."

From this passage of scripture, Ron created this amazing little prayer, and the first open is the following:

Lord, open doors. What are you asking the Lord to do when you ask him to open doors? It is to give you an opportunity to share your faith. But it's not just any opportunity; it must be a natural opportunity to bring up your relationship with Christ. Let me illustrate. Let's say you're at a gas station and you're fueling your car The person on the other side of the pump compliments your car. Would it be natural to say, "Thanks! Speaking of Jesus…" No! So the question is where did these natural opportunities come from? I believe they come from three general sources…when you have a conversation with someone about

- something going on in their life,
- something going on in your life, and
- something going on in the news.

When one of these natural opportunities occurs, the door opens for you to share your faith. So what do you do when the door opens?

Offer to pray for them right then! This may seem a little awkward, especially when you first start doing this. It does get easier as time goes by. Let's say that you're in line at Walmart. The product isn't scanning on the scanner. They call a manager over, and the manager can't find the SKU in his system. So he sends a runner to go get a similar package with a clear barcode on it. While you're waiting, the person next to you starts complaining about the problems in his life. Perfect. This is a divine appointment. You could say to the person, "I'm so sorry to hear that you're going through these struggles. When I go through struggles like you're going through, I go to my Father in heaven in prayer. He hears me and answers me. I would be honored and blessed to pray for you right now about this. Why don't we step out of line and let me pray for you, and then you can even get back in line in front of me? Do this wherever you happen to be!"

Use their first name in the prayer. This is critical. If you don't know their name, ask them for their first name so you can pray for them specifically by name. God does something in a person's heart the first time they hear their name mentioned in a prayer. Nine times out of ten, you will see tears from the person after they hear their name mentioned in the prayer. Be prepared—you'll even see tears from people you would bet money you wouldn't see tears from when you do this. I don't really have the space to do this, but I could tell you stories of big hairy biker dudes who broke down and cried when they were prayed for and their names were used. The point is to pray with them! *Nothing* will open the doors to share Christ with them than after you have prayed for them!

Lord, open hearts. God will bring you people whose hearts have been prepared, and they are receptive. Trust Him to do this.

Lord, open my mouth! Here's how I've been praying this prayer since I learned it in the fall of 2004. "Lord, open doors. Lord, open hearts. Help me to see the doors open. I don't want to miss them! Then give me the courage and boldness to open my mouth and engage these people in conversation." Pray this prayer from your heart every day, and you're going to see things you've never seen before!

Chuck Swindoll said, "Imagine the impact our churches would have in our communities if each Christian committed to sharing the Gospel once a week when someone expresses a need." Chuck is talking about the impact it could have by you sharing your faith only once a week! But what I am teaching you to do here will make you able to share your faith one, two, four, and even eight times a day! There's a Wesleyan church in the Finger Lakes of New York with an average attendance of 110 on a Sunday morning. I received a letter from the pastor of that church after I was there teaching. The letter said that the leadership team of the church realized they hadn't led a single person of Christ in six months. So they had me come to teach in January. The letter said it was a spiritual turning point for the church. In the three months since I was there, they had led twenty-five people to faith in Christ, and they were being discipled as part of their fellowship! I told that story at a different church just down the road in Elmira several years later. After telling the story, the church's pastor told me to finish the story. I told him I didn't have an ending to the story; all I had was the letter from the pastor. This pastor said that he was personal friends with the pastor of the Wesleyan church I had mentioned. That church had more than doubled in size in one year since I was there! The congregation had led over 120 people to faith in Christ! This pastor said that's why he invited me to his church to teach on that day. This can happen in your church! We just have to get serious and be obedient and start doing this.

As Cathy and I travel a lot, we eat out at restaurants very often. God is sovereign even over the restaurants that we choose to eat at and the servers we will get. I could tell you hours of stories of amazing experiences of praying for waitresses and sharing the Gospel with them. No time here. However, typically when we go to a restaurant and are greeted by our server, I will ask her name if she doesn't have a name tag on. We'll use my granddaughter's name, Maya, as an

example. When Maya returns with our drinks, I will say, "Maya, we always ask a blessing on our meal, and we always pray for our server. God selected you to be our server today. How can we pray for you today?" Don't ask "if" you can pray for the server. That will require a yes or no answer. The question is, *how* can I pray? We have had waitresses run off in tears. We have had waitresses give us multiple prayer requests. We've had waitresses run out and

meet us in the parking lot as we left the restaurant to hug us and thank us for praying for them. We've even had waitresses ask how they could pray for us! When you do this, you are showing the waitress that you were different. Now you need to tell the waitress why you're different.

What we do is bring in a Gospel of John. I especially like the one called Food for Your Soul. It has a food-themed cover. I will write a personal note in the front cover of the Gospel with the waitress's name. I usually write something like this, "Maya, thank you for the great service! This book will explain how to make *the* most important decision of your life, where you are going to spend eternity. We prayed for your request. God bless you! Don and Cathy www.donsunshine.org." Then you must leave a *great* tip...no less than 20 percent *ever*! Sadly, Christians are the cheapest tippers on planet earth! I had a waitress stand up at a training I did in Batavia, New York. She told me that she hates to work Sundays because that's when she wants to be in church worshiping her God. Her unsaved coworkers hate to work on Sundays because they work all day and make no money because that's when all of the cheap Christians come out to eat after church. She said that she had to work last Sunday. She had a table of eight Christians after church. They had great food and great service and stayed for a longtime fellowshipping. When they left, they left for a total of $2, for eight meals, slipped into a Gospel tract! When you do that, you have cheapened everything that Jesus did on the cross.

A Real-Life Illustration

We were at Daytona bike week a year ago. Four of us decided to have breakfast at the Cracker Barrel outside the Daytona International Speedway. We got a waitress named Brenda. I told her that we always ask a blessing on our meal and we always pray for our server. God had picked her to be our server that day, and I asked her how we could pray for her. Brenda asked me to pray for her son, Zachary. I asked her what his story was. She told me that he was thirteen years old. He had been born with severe birth defects. When his father saw that he had these defects, he left, and they've never heard from him since. Zachary was confined to a wheelchair. He had limited use of his hands and needed a special computer system to be educated. He was sad because he wanted to be just like any other thirteen-year-old boy. I told Brenda that we would certainly pray for her and for Zachary. When breakfast was finished, I wrote out a personal note to her in the front of the Gospel of John as I usually do. As I reached into my wallet, the other men at the table did the same thing. Without saying a word, each of us pulled out a $20 bill and stuck it in the Gospel of John. Our meals were only about $12 each. I didn't want to leave that much money in cash on the table, so I waited for Brenda to return. I handed her the Gospel of John. When she opened it up, she burst into tears. She hugged us and profusely thanked each of us for our generosity. We told her it was our pleasure to be able to help. We wish we could do more. Don't ever offer to pray for a server and leave any Gospel literature if you're not going to leave at a 20 percent tip!

The Bible is full of verses that admonish us to fear the Lord. The Scripture says that fear of the Lord is the beginning of wisdom. Fear of the Lord is also a recurring theme from Genesis through Revelation. The greatest fear shouldn't be what if I do try to rescue someone, but what will happen if I don't? There are consequences for both of us. Ron Hutchcraft told me the story of when he was in Ocean City, New Jersey, speaking at a weekend Youth Rally. One of his staff, a young lady named Jamie, went out onto the boardwalk toward the end of the evening. She leaned on the railing and was just looking out at the black Atlantic Ocean. She was listening to the surf rolling in and out and was mediating on what the Lord had done that weekend. Suddenly, she thought she heard someone cough and choke coming from the ocean. She listened again, and a woman clearly yelled for help as she was drowning. Jaimie whipped around and screamed, "Someone call 911! There's a woman drowning!" She ran down the stairs onto the sand toward the water. She stopped short of the surf, scanned back and forth, but could see nothing as it was dark. She waited to hear another sound from the woman in the water. She heard woman cough and choke again and then kicked off her shoes and ran into the surf. A man from the boardwalk followed. They dragged this woman to shore and saved her life. In the meantime, EMS, fire, and police were rolling up on the boardwalk. Ron

Hutchcraft walked out to see what all the commotion was about. Jaimie climbed up the steps in front of him soaking wet. He looked at her and asked her what happened.

Jaimie said, "I was out here minding my own business, and I heard a woman scream."

Ron asked her why she was screaming.

She said, "She was drowning!"

Ron asked what she did.

She said, "I jumped in the ocean and saved her life!"

Ron was stunned! He said that this has never happened at one of his youth rallies before and asked Jamie, "What was it like?"

Jamie explained to Ron that he didn't understand. She never swam in the ocean during the daytime because she was afraid of it. Her greatest fear was being in the ocean at night!

Ron said, "If that's your greatest fear, how were you able to do that?"

Jamie replied, "Ron, there was no one else around! I knew that if I didn't do it, she was going to drown."

Was Jamie the most qualified one to rescue her? No! But she was the closet one to that person. Question…whom are you closest to? God has put this person on your stretch of beach, not on mine and probably not your pastor's. That person is on your stretch of beach. There are people that are going to be on your stretch of beach one time… They're called divine appointments. Then there are those that are going to be on your stretch of beach multiple times. God is going to hold us responsible for each of them as watchmen on the wall. Jaimie demonstrated something called courage, which is not the absence of fear. It's just disregarding the fear. You all know that your buttons are going to get pushed. You can disable the rejection button today by not worrying about what the response is to your Gospel sharing. You can work on the other fears over time as you mature in doing this.

CHAPTER 4

Tell the Story that Can
Rescue them for Eternity

Review:

Point 1 was to recognize why you are where you are.
Point 2 was to ask Jesus every day to break your heart for the lost.
Point 3 was to conquer the fears that stop you.

4. *Tell the story that can rescue them for eternity.*

This is a combination of your personal hope story or testimony
and, if necessary, the Jesus story. Your personal hope story should
include three general parts:

- BC—"What was my life like before Christ?"
- How I was converted
- AD—"How am I different after meeting Christ?"

There needs to be a difference between your life before Christ
and your life after Christ. If there's no difference, you need to examine
yourself to be sure you're really in the faith! The Jesus story becomes
important and necessary when you encounter someone who has
never been in church. These people do not know anything about
the characters in the Bible, sin, judgment, or God's solution for the
sin problem. You will often recognize the person who has never been

in church if you ask the question, "Do you go to church?" You can believe it when someone says that they've never been in church, even down south in the Bible belt. I have challenged people and found that, in fact, they have never been in church not for a funeral, not for a wedding, not for any reason. What do you think these people know about Jesus Christ? Nothing. So you may need to go back and explain who Jesus is, why He came to earth, what He did, how He was killed on our behalf, paying our debt, how He was raised from the dead, and how they can have a relationship with their Creator God through Him.

When you share your personal hope story or testimony, you need to answer the big question, which is what difference did this make in your life? If you were just like the unsaved people at work or in your neighborhood, these people already have what you have. You're no different from them. Again, as we talked about earlier, we need to show them that we are different because we are followers of Jesus Christ.

I recognize that there are probably many people who are truly saved, but they have never shared their story with anyone. Chuck Swindoll has some suggestions for putting your story together. I would suggest typing it up in a word processor and keeping it short enough to share in a minute or less. Here's Chuck's suggestion:

Sharing Your Testimony
By Charles R. Swindoll
Acts 22:1–21

A time-honored, effective method of evangelism is your personal testimony. Just telling about your spiritual pilgrimage. The skeptic may deny your doctrine or attack your church, but he cannot honestly ignore the fact that your life has been cleaned up and revolutionized.

Now I'm not talking about some stale, dragged-out verbal marathon. That kind of testimony never attracted anyone! I'm speaking of an effective, powerful missile launched from your lips to the ears of the unsaved. Consider these five suggestions:

1. *You want to be listened to, so be interesting.* It's a contradiction to talk about how exciting Christ really is in an uninteresting way. Remember to guard against religious clichés, jargon, and hard-to-understand terminology. Theologians, beware!

2. *You want to be understood, so be logical.* Think of your salvation in three phases and construct your testimony accordingly: (a) before you were born again—the struggles within, the loneliness, lack of peace, absence of love, unrest, and fears; (b) the decision that revolutionized your life; and (c) the change—the difference it has made since you received Christ.

3. *You want the moment of your new birth to be clear, so be specific.* Don't be vague. Speak of Christ, not the church. Emphasize faith more than feeling. Be simple and direct as you describe what you did or what you prayed or what you said. This is crucial!

4. *You want your testimony to be used, so be practical.* Be human and honest as you talk. Don't promise, "All your problems will end if you will become a Christian," for that isn't true. Try to think as unbelievers think.

5. *You want your testimony to produce results, so be warm and genuine.* A smile breaks down more barriers than the hammer blows of cold, hard facts. Let your enthusiasm flow freely. It's hard to convince someone of the sheer joy and excitement of knowing

Christ if you're wearing a face like a jail warden. Above all, be positive and courteous.
Absolutely refuse to argue. Nobody I ever
met was "arm wrestled" into the kingdom.
Insults and put-downs turn people off.

Ask God to open your lips and honor your
words...but be careful! Once your missile hits
the target, you'll become totally dissatisfied with
your former life as an earthbound, secret-service
saint.

*No persuasive technique will ever take the
place of your personal testimony. If you have not
discovered the value of telling others how God rear-
ranged your life, you've missed a vital link in the
chain of His plan for reaching the lost.*

In John 9, we read the story of the blind man whom Jesus
healed. Everyone in Jerusalem knew this man was blind. When Jesus
healed him, even the religious leaders and Pharisees knew that he
had been healed. However, they were so bent on getting this man to
say something they could use against Jesus as an excuse to kill Him
that they brought him into the synagogue and questioned him. They
didn't like his answers, so they brought his parents in. The Bible says
his parents were afraid that they would be put out of the synagogue if
they told the truth. So they told the Jewish leaders that their son was
an adult and they should ask him how he was healed. You can read
the conversation that occurs between him and the religious leaders.
I don't know about you, but I think he smiled through the whole
thing. He gave God all the glory! And the religious leaders didn't like
it. The wanted him to say that Jesus was a sinner. The former blind
man replied, "Whether he's a sinner or not, I don't know. One thing
I do know. I was blind, but now I see!" The blind man showed an
incredible difference that Jesus had made in his life. Every one of you
has a story. Do not let the devil lie to you and tell you that your story
has no value. I was an Eagle Scout, raised Catholic, who want to be

a cop. How bad of a kid you think I was growing up? I never drank alcohol. I never smoked. I never took drugs. And God uses my story to impact in people's lives, and he can use yours as well.

Based on the story of the blind man, here is a pattern for sharing your story. This is who I was: I was blind, helpless, and hopelessly lost in my sin. Then I met Jesus. This is how we changed my life. No one could argue with your story. It is *your* story. The *Life Application Study Bible*'s commentary on 1 Corinthians 1:17 says, "You don't have to be a great speaker with a large vocabulary to share the good news effectively. The persuasive power is in the story not in the storyteller."

If you encounter someone who's never been in church, tell them the Jesus story so they understand. Also, it is important that when we share the Gospel with a lost person that we say it in words they can understand. Ron Hutchcraft has a term for the language church people use. He calls our language Christianese, the language of Christians. You see, we use biblical words that we have been taught and understand because we've been educated in Sunday school classes, Bible studies, and church sermons. When we use these words with a person who has never been in church, you might as well be speaking in Hebrew because they're not going to understand a word you're saying. So if you use any of these biblical Christianese words when sharing the Gospel, you must be sensitive to the fact that they may not understand what you're saying. So you'll need to use as few of these words as possible, and when you use any of these words, be prepared to define the words for the lost person. What are some of these Christianese words that we would use to share the plan of salvation with someone who has lost that they might not understand?

- Born again—Nicodemus, the religious leader, didn't understand this term when Jesus used it.
- Lost
- Saved
- Repent
- Sin
- Savior

- Faith
- My favorite—washed in the blood! Hint: don't start a conversation with a lost person telling them they need to be "washed in the blood." It could get ugly.

Ron Hutchcraft has a way of sharing the Gospel in four sentences with no Christianese words. Now I ruined it by adding four Christianese words at the end, and you'll understand why when we get to that point.

Also, you need to stick to Jesus. For two thousand years, the command from hell has been "edit out Jesus." David Platt said, "When we spread the seed, it is important to remember that the issue has always been and continues to be today the name of Jesus. All through the book of Acts, the apostles insist on saying, "You need to come in the name of Jesus. That's where salvation is. There's no other name." And what did the religious leaders say? "You can talk all you want. Just don't talk about the name of Jesus." See the devil doesn't care if we talk about church or religion or God or family values or love. He hates the name of Jesus. Don't say *Jesus*! Why? Because it's the name by which people are saved. It's the name at which according to Philippians 2 "every knee shall bow, including every demon."

When someone asks me what church I go to, I say, "I go to a Bible-believing church." After I have successfully planted the Gospel seed in the person's heart, then I'll brag on my church, my pastor, and all of the things I love about my church. If all you do is talk about your church and you never get to the Gospel, you failed. The person will walk away knowing lots about your church and why you love it but nothing about how to be saved. Don't put the cart before the horse. Paul said in 1 Corinthians 2:2, "For I resolved nothing while I was with you except Jesus Christ and him crucified." That's what you want to focus on. Your church comes after that.

Remember, inviting someone to church is not a substitute for you sharing your faith. Nowhere in the Bible does it tell us to invite people to church. We are to share the Gospel and make disciples. I live in East Tennessee. Tennessee is an amazing place because everyone thinks they are already a Christian! But when you get down to talking about a person's faith, it becomes very obvious that they are not Christians; they only think they are. In the four and a half years I have lived in Tennessee, I invited a number of lost people to come to my church. I have yet to be successful. Very few people will come to your church if you invite them. So you have to be sure to share the Gospel with them *before* you invite them to church. Otherwise, you fail the assignment of planting or watering the Gospel seed in their heart.

What if someone disagrees with you when you're sharing the Gospel? That's okay. Not everyone is going to agree with what you're saying. But your goal should be to just tell them what the Bible says. If you're interested in challenging them, you might ask them what they believe and after hearing it, ask them what their source of information is and how they know it's true. You should be able to justify your beliefs fairly easily.

When sharing the Gospel message, you want to tell them of life's most important relationship. Here's Ron Hutchcraft's way of doing it:

There's a relationship you were created to have. It makes sense if you think about it logically. God is eternal, and He is the Creator. We are His creation, and we will live eternally. It doesn't make any sense logically that He would create an eternal being unless He wanted to spend eternity with that being. Colossians 1:16 says, "All things were created by him and for him" referring to *Jesus Christ.*

It's a relationship you don't have. You might be thinking, "Hold on, Don. That doesn't make any sense. You just said there was a relationship I was created to have. So why don't I have it?" The reason is sin. Remember in Colossians it said that we were created for Him. The problem is that we have lived for *us!* There is a little word to describe that, which is sin. Now you've used a Christianese word. So you must be able to define it. I'll give you two simple definitions that anyone can understand. First, spell it. S-i-n. If you take off the *S* and you take off the *N*, what's left? *I.* "I" am running my life. "I" am making the decisions. "I" am in charge. God's not telling me what to do. Another simple definition of sin is "Running your life instead of letting God run it." According to Isaiah 59:2, "Your sins have separated you from your God" for all of eternity. When speaking with someone about the Gospel, you must deal with the sin issue somehow before you present a solution. If a doctor offers a patient a cure for a disease that the patient doesn't know he has, it makes no sense. But if the patient is aware of the fact that he has a deadly disease and the doctor offers him the cure for that disease, then it makes total sense, and the patient wants it.

In our society today, it seems like people need to be made aware of the fact that the Bible says if we are guilty of breaking one of God's laws, we are just as guilty as a person who is broken all of God's laws. James 2:10 says that.

I can't tell you how many times that when I've asked the person if they were to die suddenly today where they would spend eternity, the answer that they gave me was, "Heaven." When I asked them why they thought they should be in heaven, they said because they are a very good person. When someone says they are very good person, who are they comparing themselves to? Someone who is a far worse than them! Is that all that's required? I just have to beat out some mass murderer to get into heaven? No. So how do you deal with someone in this situation?

A Real-Life Illustration

Let me illustrate with another true story. My friends Ron and Charlie were with me at Daytona Bike Week. We went to a restaurant where we often ate breakfast. On this particular day, we got there a little late. The restaurant was full, and there were three people in front of us in line to get into the restaurant. Ron saw that the waitresses were clearing a round table that could seat six people. I believe the Holy Spirit prompted Ron to ask the three people in front of us if we could share a table with them for breakfast, because he did. The three people agreed that we could share the table with him. We sat down with Bruce, Julie, and Tristan, all members of the same family. Tristan owned an HVAC company, and Mom and Dad worked for her. Dad did installations, and last October, he had a three-thousand-pound air conditioner fall on his leg, and it snapped it like a twig. He was just getting ready to start rehab. Mom handled the accounting for the business. We got a prayer request from our server and asked each of three people how we could pray for them as well. We included them in our prayers and ate our breakfast. In the course of conversation, one of us asked them the question, "If you were to die suddenly today, where would you spend eternity?" Julie blurted out, "I know for sure that I would go to heaven." One of us asked her how she knew that. She replied, "Because I'm a very, very good person." Again, one of us asked, "Can we put that to the test?" She said, "Sure."

Each of us took turns asking her questions from the "Way of the Master" training. These questions center around four of the Ten Commandments.

One of us asked Julie if she ever told lies. Julie replied, "Of course I've told lies. Everyone has." She was then asked, "What do you call someone who tells lies?" She said, "A liar."

She was then asked if she ever stole anything regardless of value. She replied, "I guess I've taken something from time to time." The next question was, "So what are you called if you've taken something that didn't belong to you?" She replied, "A thief."

Julie was then asked if she's ever lusted after someone. She said, "Yes. Every week there are hot guys who come into the shop." We explained to her that Jesus said if she's done that, she's already committed adultery with that person in her heart. So she was an adulterer at heart.

Julie was then asked if she's ever used God's name in vain. She replied, "Yeah, I swear like a drunken sailor pretty much every day." We explained that the Bible calls that blasphemy.

So we summarized, "Julie, by your own admission, you're a lying, thieving, adulterer at heart who blasphemes God. You're batting four for four on the Ten Commandments. If we were to question you on the other six, you'd be as guilty as me, because I failed the test too!"

"Julie, if God were to judge you by the Ten Commandments, would you be innocent or guilty?" She responded, "Guilty."

So would you go to heaven or hell? Boom! All four faces instantly changed. She said, "Now you have me scared." We again asked for an answer, and she said she was afraid to give us her answer. We waited, and she finally said, "Hell."

We told her that she was right. We then asked her if that concerned her, and she said it did. We then went on to explain what Jesus did for her so she wouldn't have to go to hell.

We prayed for each of them and gave them each a Gospel of John with the plan of salvation inside. When we got up to leave, they each gave us the longest hugs and profusely thanked us for having breakfast with them and telling the about the forgiveness that is available to them through Jesus Christ. In my opinion, there is no better way to deal with the sin issue than by using four of God's Ten Commandments. It is a standalone Gospel presentation that you can use if start by asking the question, "If you were to die today, where would you spend eternity?" You can learn how to do this at www.wayofthemaster.com.

The problem is that when God created us, He wanted to have control of our lives. When we spiritually hijack control of our lives, it carries an eternal death sentence in a very real place called hell. Romans 5:23 tells us, "For the wages of sin is death."

The good news is that...

It's a relationship you can have. I don't have it because of what I did. I *can* have it because of what Jesus did. John 3:16 is a great introductory verse to the Gospel, "For God so loved the world that he gave his one and only son, that whoever believes in him shall not perish, but have eternal life." If you choose to quote this verse for a person you're sharing with, you can make it personal by saying, "For God so loved _____ (insert their name here)..."

It's a relationship you must choose to have. You can't acquire this relationship by going to church, being baptized, teaching Sunday school, or volunteering to serve at VBS. You get this relationship because you *choose* to have it.

Here's a true story from American history. A man named George Wilson was convicted of killing a federal guard during an armed robbery in the 1800s. He was sentenced to death by hanging. While he was sitting in prison, awaiting his execution date, a US President left office. As is the custom, this US President decided to pardon some prisoners. One of those prisoners who received a pardon was George Wilson. A guard brought the pardon to George in his cellblock and said, "George, I have great news for you! You just received a pardon signed by the president of the United States! You are a free man! We are going to give you a suit of clothes and some money and take you to town. You get to start your life over!" George read the pardon, handed it back to the guard, said, "I don't want it," and sat on his bunk. The guard was stunned! He asked George if he actually read the document. George said, "I don't want it, and you can't make me leave." The guard didn't know what to do. So he took it to a supervisor, and the supervisor couldn't convince George to leave either. This went all the way up the chain of command to the warden of the prison, who made a personal visit to George in his cell. He also couldn't convince George to leave voluntarily. The warden was unsure of what to do. He decided to write a letter to the governor of the state and ask for guidance. When the governor read the letter, he laughed to himself and was shocked that this man would not leave prison when he was given a pardon by the president United States. The governor told the story to the newspaper people, who wrote an article about George Wilson, because this has never happened in American history. A group of people got together, I think, the predecessors to our present-day ACLU; and they filed suit against George Wilson. They said that he had to accept the pardon that was signed by the President because it was just like a law. George got a court-appointed attorney and fought it all the way back to the US Supreme Court. Here's what they ruled, "The value of the pardon is determined by the one receiving the pardon." So if George didn't want to accept it for himself, he didn't have to. So he chose not to except it, and when his execution date came around, they hung him. Now did George believe a pardon existed? Sure, he did! But he didn't choose to accept for himself.

The same thing is true with the pardon that God offers every one of us, as his created human beings. But we must individually decide whether we will choose to accept the pardon for ourselves or not. The next logical question is, how do I do that?

We do that by doing three things. These are Christianese words. You must be able to define these words simply for the people you are sharing with.

Believe. You must believe that Jesus Christ was the Son of God, He died in your place, and was raised from the dead. This is foundational. There is plenty of historical evidence of Jesus of His life on planet earth, His death, burial, and resurrection. After He was raised from the dead, He was seen by more than five hundred people at a time over a period of forty days. It is an historical fact not even the Jewish religious leaders of the day could refute. Folks, that's awesome!

It is very important to recognize that *profession of faith does not always equal possession of faith.* I live in East Tennessee. Tennessee is an amazing state because everybody that I've ever met here believes they are already a Christian! Now if you drill down a little bit in conversation, you're going to find out that they have a very skewed view of what being a Christian is all about. R. C. Sproul said, "It is the *possession* of faith, not the *profession* of faith that transfers us from the kingdom of darkness to the kingdom of light."

When I began trying to share my faith in Christ, I was scared to death. When I began the conversation and the person said they were already a Christian, my heart rate and breathing would return to normal, and the sweating would stop, and I'd say, "That's great! Nice meeting you!" I'd walk away not feeling very good, but I tried, right? Then I started to realize that if a person is not a Jew, a Buddhist, a Hindu, a Muslim, a Jehovah's Witness, or a Mormon, they believe they are a Christian by default. I mean we live in a Christian nation, right? So this is very important. When someone says they are already a Christian, don't believe them. You must lovingly challenge them saying something like, "That's great! Tell me how it happened!" Or "That's great! Tell me your story!" You will know within five or ten seconds whether they are or aren't based on what they say. Then you'll know what to do next.

A Real-Life Illustration

I needed a trailer to trailer motorcycles from our home in Pennsylvania to South Carolina to go to Daytona Bike Week. We would drive to Columbia, South Carolina, and park our truck and trailer at a pastor friend's house and then ride our motorcycles the rest away to Florida. I found a suitable trailer for sale in Hellertown, Pennsylvania, on Craigslist. I met with a man named Kip, and we agreed on a price to purchase the trailer. As we were driving to the notary to change the title, this conversation occurred.

Kip said, "So you have a ministry."

I replied, "Yes."

He said, "That's pretty cool. My uncle was a missionary to Brazil."

I said, "That's neat."

He said, "Yeah it wasn't very lucrative, but I guess it was rewarding."

I said, "Well, that's an interesting this to say, Kip. What do you believe?"

Kip replied, "I'm a Christian."

I said, "That's great! Tell me how it happened."

Kip Said, "Well, when I was a little boy, my mom worked at a Christian Camp every summer."

I replied, "And…"

Kip said, "And I got to go every summer for free."

I replied, "And…"

Kip said, "And what?"

I said, "Kip, can I tell you what the Bible says?"

We had a long, detailed conversation about the plan of salvation, and I answered a lot of spiritual questions that he had. I gave him some Gospel literature to read, and I left.

George Barna did a survey of self-professing born-again Christians in April 2011. What he found was disturbing, and I would suggest it is even worse today. Twenty-five percent believe in universalism. That is becoming very popular today. That means that everyone goes to heaven; no one goes to hell. That is clearly not what the Bible teaches. Another 24 percent believe that it doesn't matter what faith you follow. You're still going to end up in heaven. Again, not what the Bible teaches. And lastly, almost half, 40 percent, believe that Muslims and Christians worship the same God! Sorry! Nothing could be further from the truth!

Let me continue by illustrating with some statistics. When I go into a church to teach people how to be obedient to Christ by sharing their faith and making disciples, on Saturdays, we average only 10 percent of the average Sunday morning attendance. I realize that some small percentage had to work. Some small percentage had a family commitment, or they were ill. But that's not 90 percent consistently over six hundred presentations in twenty-seven states. There's something wrong with this picture.

About 51 percent is the minimum percentage to make a majority. What would say a "vast" majority might be percentage-wise—75, 80, 95? I'm sure we'd all agree that it's a *big* number. Some quotes for you. The late Dr. D. James Kennedy said this, "The vast majority of the members of our churches are not Christians. I say this without the slightest fear of contradiction. I base it on the empirical evidence of examining thousands of people's lives over twenty-four years." John MacArthur, in his book *Hard to Believe*, said this," I believe that the church in America is jammed full of people who think they are Christians, and they don't know that they're not. They've jumped on the Jesus bandwagon, thinking everything is swell, and they're going to be seriously surprised at the judgment." A little later on in his book, he said that "The greatest mission field in our country is in our churches." Billy Graham said this, "I would be thrilled if 5 percent of all the people who came down over the years during my crusades were truly saved." He thinks the vast majority is 95 percent, and they're not! What if these men are right? That means the tens of millions of Americans attending church every Sunday are lost and going to hell, and I happen to believe they're right. If you are being disobedient to the commandment of Jesus Christ to make disciples, which begins with you telling someone about your faith, and some dude without any special education or skills is coming to your church to show you in just four hours how easy it is to begin doing this, what could be more important? Yet only 10 percent of the church will make the commitment to come for four hours and learn how to be obedient. I can't help but question the authenticity of their salvation experience. Many people believe they became Christians by simply repeating the words of a prayer. Repentance was never mentioned, nor was it a part of the decision-making process. I believe a lot of these people missed one key step in the salvation process…and that step is to

Repent—the person must be willing to repent. The word repent occurs seventy-eight times in sixty-six books of the Bible. If you look up the simple definition in a concordance, it occurs so many times, on so many pages. I didn't count how many times, and it occurred in three columns on every page. It's a theme from Genesis all the way through the book of Revelation. When John the Baptist began his ministry, the very first word out of his mouth was *repent*. When Jesus went into the wilderness for forty days to be tempted by Satan and came out to start his earthly ministry, the very first word out of his mouth was *repent*. See if you can wiggle through this: Jesus Himself said in Luke 13:3 and repeats Himself in Luke 13:5, "Unless you repent you too will all perish." So why would I ever leave that out of a Gospel presentation? Yet it is left out most of the time. Salvation hinges on repentance, yet it is often left out in most Gospel literature and most Gospel presentations. Acts 26:20 is just one of the many passages that speaks of the need to repent. It reads, "That all must repent of their sins and turn to God—and prove they have changed by the good things they do."

Being that salvation hinges on a repentant heart, I wanted to understand this fully. Many people think that the Bible is written in English, and the people in Bible times all spoke with British accents… Have you ever noticed this? The Bible was actually written in Greek, Aramaic, and Hebrew. In Luke 13:3 and Luke 13:5, the word for *repent* is actually the Greek word *metanoia*. I asked and confirmed with several people who know a lot more than me to define that word. When I understood what it meant, I became concerned. When Jesus said, "Unless you metanoia what did He mean? Metanoia has four necessary components. You have to get all four. Three out of four on a quiz in school is a 75 or a C. This is pass/fail. Metanoia means a change of

Mind—we make up our minds that we are not going to sin and rebel against God anymore. We are going to make up our minds to live in obedience.

Heart—the decision we make with our mind has to drop fourteen inches into our heart, which is where conversion takes place, according to Romans 10:9–10. It's a heart's decision.

Life—your life will change. You will not be living a lifestyle like the lost world does.

Purpose—your purpose for being on the planet will change. What was my purpose for being on earth *before* coming to faith in Christ?

- A good job
- Good salary
- Nice house
- Nice car
- Good food
- Beautiful family
- Vacations
- Recreation
- Retirement

How does this change when I become a follower of Jesus Christ? Remember, you were previously a slave to sin. God purchased you with the precious holy blood of His Son, Jesus Christ. He *owns* you now. You belong to Him! You have a new Master, and it is not you! You become a slave of Christ as several epistle writers described themselves. With this new Master or Lord, I need to do whatever He tells me to do. That's the difference.

Chuck Swindoll wrote, "Paul wants to be clear that the repentance he's preaching isn't symbolic—it's a wholesale rearrangement of one's priorities that produces change." Colossians 2:6 says, "And now, just as you accepted Christ Jesus as you Lord, you must continue to follow him." Please notice the verse didn't say you accepted Jesus as your "Savior." It said *Lord.* You see, we throw the word *Lord* around in conversations and in prayer and don't even consider what it really means. You're acknowledging His ownership of your life when you call Him Lord. The word *Lord* occurs hundreds of times in the Scriptures. In the Greek, it is the word *Kurios*, which means "Master, Owner, Someone in control of someone else."

David Platt wrote, "Surely none of us can decide to make Him Lord. Jesus is Lord regardless of what you or I decide…the question is not whether we will make Jesus our Lord. The real question is whether you or I will submit to His Lordship, and this is the essence of salvation."

Kyle Idleman wrote, "A fan is an enthusiastic admirer. I wonder sometimes if our churches have become stadiums for fans. Are you a fan or a follower? There is no salvation without surrender." Churches in America are full of Jesus fans. Sadly, fans aren't going to heaven. Only followers are going to heaven. There is a big difference between the two. Jesus has plenty of fans; what He needs is more followers. Which one are you?

Chuck Swindoll wrote, "Jesus Christ has the right to rule over me. So when He applies His rulership and leads me to a certain direction, I do not resist and I do not wrestle. I go, I do, I obey, I say no to what I want because He is in charge. He rules my life. I obey Him. I acknowledge that He has the right to rule over me. He is not only Savior, but He is also Lord…and as the Lord, He's in charge."

When I consider the four components of the word *metanoia*, it sounds a lot like *Lordship* because I can't come up with a fifth component category. We are surrendering *all* to Him. Therefore, it is impossible to call someone Lord and then not do what that person commands. In Luke 6:46, Jesus made the same point. He said, "And why do you call me Lord, Lord and not do the things I say?" So the Lordship question is, "Have you ever surrendered your life to the Lordship of Jesus Christ in repentance and faith and committed to follow Him for the rest of your life?" That's what being born again is all about!

This may shock you. Do you realize that no one in the Bible ever got saved by praying a prayer? Nowhere in the Scriptures do you ever see someone say, "Just pray this prayer" or "Repeat after me." We all know people who "prayed the prayer," and their lives never changed, but they're convinced they have fire insurance for all of eternity. As it says in Romans, it's a heart decision, and only God can examine a heart. David Jeremiah said this, "Where there is no Spiritual fruit, there is no Spiritual life." That's a bold statement but absolutely true!

I believe there are three kinds of believers. They are the following:

True believers—who have surrendered their lives to the Lordship of Jesus Christ in repentance and faith. They are following Jesus when everyone is looking and when no one is looking.

Unbelievers—this is the easiest group to identify. They are all around us, and we can identify them by the fruit in their lives. They aren't following Jesus.

The last group is the toughest group to identify, and I would submit that our churches are full of this third group. This group of people is going to hear what I believe are the seven scariest words in the Bible from Matthew 7. They are going to stand for Christ on judgment day and give amazing reasons why He should let them into heaven: "Lord, I cast out demons in Your Name! Lord, I healed the sick in Your Name!" Jesus's response is chilling. "Depart from me I never knew you." It's too late at this point. You can't have a do-over. You can't have five extra minutes to make things right. Your eternity is sealed. You were headed for hell. I called this group the…

Make-believers—sadly, I do believe our churches are full of make-believers.

The question is, which one are you? I don't know which one you are. Only God and you know the truth. My goal in life is to take as many nonbelievers and make-believers to heaven with me as I can. I hope yours is too.

Lastly, the third step in the salvation process, and the Christianese word we need to define is...

Receive—that means that you are going to place all of your faith and trust in Christ alone to save you. You fall at the cross morally bankrupt and tell God that that you have no way to pay the tremendous debt that's due when you die and that you'd like Jesus to pay it for you. Romans 3:22 says, "We are made right with God by placing our faith in Jesus Christ."

To summarize the points of the Gospel message:
There's a relationship you were created to have.
It's a relationship you don't have.
It's a relationship you can have.
But you must choose to have it.

How do you choose? Be able to define these Christianese terms when you use them.

Believe,
Repent, and
Receive.

Over the years, many people have come to our live events, believing they were saved and then finding out that they weren't. In fact, over 1,600 people have given their lives to Jesus Christ at our live events. This was not expected. The Gospel message has been so watered down that when people are confronted with the true Gospel, the Holy Spirit convicts them, and they make a real decision. I don't know where you stand. Has the Holy Spirit been speaking to your heart as you read this book? If so, please don't ignore His prompting. Make things right. With all of your heart, surrender your life on planet earth to the Lordship of Jesus Christ. Repent, that means change your mind, heart, life, and purpose for being here. Place all of your faith in Jesus Christ's death, burial, and resurrection, and commit to follow Him while you're still walking on planet earth.

Also, if you'd be interested in having me come to help equip your church, please let me know. My contact information is as follows:

P—(484) 332-0373
E—don@donsunshine.org
W—www.donsunshine.org

CHAPTER 5

Ambassador Journal Entries— Real-Life Examples

I haven't been writing up the most recent divine appointments, as I have gone high-tech, and I have been doing a YouTube vlog instead. However, below are some of the stories that I had journaled prior to doing the videos. I hope they will be an encouragement to you and that by reading them, they will open your eyes to the divine appointments that God already has planned for you going forward.

You can view the vlog on YouTube. Search for "Don Sunshine Ministries vlog," and click Follow.

The Sovereignty of God and a Divine Appointment

A while ago, while visiting my daughter in Pennsylvania, a neighbor backed into my truck and did about $4,500 worth of damage to the driver's side rear of the truck. After returning home, I had the truck repaired, and when I went to pick it up, we discovered that the driver's side exhaust pipe and been pushed in and bent. This wasn't clearly visible when I initially brought the truck in. The body shop tried to straighten it but was unsuccessful, so they sent me to the local Meineke shop to have it looked at (the sovereignty of God). I had a nice conversation with the Meineke manager on a number of topics before he looked at the truck. After checking the exhaust, he said he'd need the truck for two to three hours to heat and bent the exhaust pipe back to where it belonged. As he exited my truck, his cell phone holder got caught on something and broke. He had an Otter box just like the one I had for my phone before purchasing my current phone. I told him that I had the same Otterbox and the belt clip that he had just broken. I told him that I had never used the belt clip and I'd be happy to give it to him if he wanted it. He was very excited and grateful and thanked me for offering. I told him that when I returned to have the truck worked on, I'd bring it to him and he could have it. I was able to share the Gospel with him, and I gave him a *One Second After You... Die"* booklet to read.

I then returned to the body shop, and we made an appointment to have the exhaust repaired this afternoon. I brought the Otterbox belt clip with me and gave it to the manager. He again thanked me, and I told him that after he read the booklet I gave him to please call me if he had any questions. He agreed to do that. I wished him a Merry Christmas and returned home. Praise God for another divine appointment!

*****

This morning, I went to our weekly men's Bible study at Chick-fil-A, and there were two *very large* police officers having breakfast there. I went over, introduced myself, and told them that I was a police officer on a SWAT team in New Jersey years ago. I shared a "Police Lives Matter" Gospel card with each of them and asked if I could pray for them. They were so excited and grateful that I would do this for them. I got their first names, put one hand on each of their shoulders, and prayed for their safety and salvation. They thanked me again, and I joined our Bible study group.

*****

Months and months ago, I signed up to be an Uber driver to pick up some spending money. There is very little need for that in Jonesborough, Tennessee, and I have never received a ride request.

But today I got my first call. I went to Walmart and picked up Dawn and her boyfriend, Mike, loaded their shopping bags in the car, and drove them home. I asked some questions about them; and as we arrived at their home, I shared the Gospel with them, gave them a Gospel of John, and asked if and how I could pray for them. They each gave me something to pray about, and I did. I then helped carry their packages into their house and headed home. It was a very short ride but clearly a divine appointment.

*****

Cathy and I went grocery shopping this afternoon. While standing in line, I received a phone call from a lady in Danville, Virginia. She said she was coming to the MAD Live Event I was doing this Saturday in Lynchburg, Virginia, and wanted to know if it was appropriate to bring her nine-year-old son. I explained to her that I do the same training for Christian middle schools that I will be doing on Saturday and that I have testimonies of the parents of two seven-year-olds and a ten-year-old who attended the event and put what they learned into practice. She got very excited and said she'd also bring her daughter. She thanked me for answering the phone and hung up. The lady in line in front of me apparently heard the conversation and asked what I would be doing and could she send her grandkids to the event. I told her I would be teaching "lifestyle evangelism," and she asked what that was. I explained I would be teaching people how to share their faith in Christ every day. I then asked her what she believed. She told me she believed in God because that's the only way she has survived raising three grandkids while her daughter was in jail, but she doesn't go to church. I asked her if she had ever made the decision to turn from her sins, surrender her life to Christ, begin to follow Him, and trust Him by faith. She said no. I explained that this decision was the most important decision of her life. I gave her a Gospel of John and explained what it was, and I asked if she knew where Mt. Zion Baptist was located. She said she did as she had gone there at some point in the past to take advantage of the food pantry. I strongly invited her to come to church and bring the grandkids. I also gave her my business card so she could contact me if she had questions or needed more information.

What a perfect illustration of the sovereignty of God! Had this lady from Virginia not called me when she did, I would not have had that conversation while standing in line next to this woman. That perfect timing gave me the opportunity to share the Gospel with her. This was a perfect illustration of the first point in my training, "recognize why you are where you are." Praise God for His perfect timing and sovereignty!

After unloading the groceries at home, the Schwann's guy came by and commented how much he liked the Indian motorcycle in our garage. I asked him if he rode and said he did. He has an Ultra Classic, so we talked about motorcycles for a little while. Then I asked if I could share something with him. He said yes. I reached into the bag on the Indian and pulled out a Gospel of John and shared the plan of salvation with him. He agreed to take it home and read it. This has been a good day.

*****

Yesterday, we kicked off our new off-road ministry. I went to Windrock Park just south of us to ride and share the Gospel with people God connected me with. I went to the general store to register and get my permit. As I pulled into the parking lot, there was only one vehicle there. It was a nice Ford F-250 with PA tags and a trailer attached. After coming back out to unload our machine, the man and his son were doing the same. I asked where they were from in Pennsylvania and he said, "Pittsburgh." We walked for a while and found out that Gary and his sixteen-year-old son, Gavin, were there for a day of riding. He mentioned it was his first time at Windrock, and I said the same. He told me that the lady behind the counter gave him a one-page sheet with a suggested three-hour loop ride that was easy to do. I didn't get one of them, I asked if I could follow them on the loop. They agreed. We stopped several times and returned to the parking area for lunch.

We talked further over lunch and agreed on doing another short loop after lunch. As they had Gary to navigate and Gavin to drive, they mapped out another route which included a fun moderate rated trail. We did that loop, had a nice ride, and returned to the parking area. I asked if Gary had a business card with him, and he regrettably said, "No, they're in the hotel." I gave him my card and asked if he went to church. He said he was raised Catholic but had issues with some of the church teachings. I shared my story with him and then told him that he could be assured of going to heaven when he died. I shared the Gospel message with him and gave both of them a Gospel of John with the plan of salvation outlined in the front of the booklet. I also gave him a *One Second After You... Die* booklet and asked if I could pray for both of them. Gary excitedly said, "Yes!" I called Gavin over and asked if anyone had ever prayed for him, and he said he knew his mom did. I told him that I wanted to pray for him and his dad, so I placed one hand on each of their shoulders and prayed for their salvation, safe riding tomorrow and a safe ride home. He thanked me again and again, and I invited them to come to the MAD Live Event that I'll be doing in Beaver Falls, Pennsylvania, in a few weeks. Gary said their weekends were pretty busy with part-time business that they have. I suggested that God might open the day up so they could attend. We'll see what the Lord has in mind. What a great way to start this new phase of ministry the Lord has opened up!

*****

I arrived at our hotel before our annual meeting tomorrow. After unloading the luggage cart, I headed to the elevator. A lady got off the elevator just before I reached it and was walking down the hallway in the same direction I was headed. She had a limp, was walking with a cane, and was dragging a rolling suitcase and carrying another bag. I entered the elevator and returned the luggage cart to the lobby. As the elevator doors opened at my floor, she was walking past the elevator going in the opposite direction. I commented that I had just seen her walking in the other direction. She then asked if room 327 was in the new direction she was walking, and I said, "Yes!" I asked if I could help her carry her bags and she gratefully said, "Yes!" I took the rolling suitcase and the bag she was carrying, and we walked down the hall. She said she had just arrived after a ten-hour drive from Illinois, and I told her we had just arrived after a nine-hour drive from Tennessee. We talked a little more, and she unlocked the door to her room. I brought the luggage in and set it down. She thanked me again, and I left. I had given out the one Gospel I had in my pocket earlier at dinner, but I had more literature in my room. So I retrieved a *One Second After You... Die* booklet and returned to her room. I knocked at the door, she answered it, and I asked if I could share something with her that had changed my life and eternity. She excitedly agreed, and I explained what the booklet was about and asked if she would accept it and read it. She smiled and said, "Yes! This is probably exactly what I need to read after the trip from H-E double hockeysticks." We smiled and said goodbye. It's all about God's timing. It was perfect!

*****

Today I dropped a bunch of flattened boxes off at the local dump. I took the backroads from there to Best Buy to pick up Cathy's desktop computer. On the way, I saw a young black Angus calf on the shoulder of the road next to a barbed wire fenced in area. I was concerned the little guy would wonder into the road and get filet'd. So I turned the car around and went back. He didn't care for my presence, and he was wondering around the fenced-in area trying to find a way back inside. I stopped at the house above the cattle, and no one answered the door. The driveway to the house was shared by a home way up the hill. So I drove up there and knocked at the door. A lady named Debbie came to the door, and I asked if she had anything to do with the cattle at the bottom of her driveway. She said, "Yes!" I told her what I had seen, and she got in her car and hurried down the hill. Her mom pulled into the driveway as she got out of the car and started walking toward the cattle. They quickly moved away from her, and the little guys somehow got under the single strand of electrified barbed wire and went back inside the fenced-in area. Debbie and her mom thanked me over and over for taking the time to stop and let them know what was happening with the calf. I asked if I could share something with them, and they agreed. I gave each of them a Gospel of John with the plan of salvation in the front and shared Christ with them, and they agreed to read it.

Two Divine Appointments Today

This morning, I returned my rental car and was driven home by a nice young man named JP. I had some spiritual conversations with him before, but this time we got down to the "guts" of the Gospel. In the course of conversation, he told me that he had prayed a prayer twice and thought he was a Christian, but he had never repented. He had some doubts about the Bible after watching some "documentaries" on cable stations. It didn't help that he had a Muslim roommate who also beat up on the Bible. I shared with him how he could be confident that the Bible is the Word of God, a supernatural book, and explained the plan of salvation to him. I also asked if I could pray for him, and he let me lay my hand on his shoulder and pray for his salvation. JP told me that he wanted to pick me up the next time I needed a ride so we could talk some more. That will be Thursday. I gave him two booklets to read, and he indicated he wants to come to the Bible study that I plan on doing. Praise God! I have a little mission field with most of the enterprise staff here!

This evening, I went to Buffalo Wild Wings in Johnson City to pick up some dinner to go. Tuesday is half-price day on wings. About seven young ladies were standing around the register. They were all waitresses. One of them engaged me in a conversation and asked how my Halloween was, and I replied, "Not great." She asked, "Why?" I told her that I was returning from a long trip to Rochester and Buffalo, New York. Her name was Erica, and she asked what I was doing up there. I told her that I spoke at a men's conference on Saturday and taught in a church in Lockport on Sunday. Erica asked me what I taught, and I told her, "Lifestyle evangelism." She said, "I'm from upstate New York!" I asked, "Where?" She said, "Alfred." I told her that I knew exactly where that was because I lived in the Finger Lakes and worked for Family Life. She got all excited and told me that she had listened to the station from time to time. I asked where she went to church. She told me that she went to Alfred Almond Bible Church because Pastor Prince's daughter and she shared the same birthday and were best friends. I told her that I had taught my evangelism training in Pastor Prince's church nine years ago. I asked how she got to Tennessee. She told me her dad moved here three years ago for work, and she is now a freshman at ETSU. I asked where she goes to church now, and she told me she doesn't go at all. I asked her why, and she said she heard a guest speaker at Alfred Almond Bible Church who said something that she didn't like. Basically, he just said that anyone who didn't "believe like he believed" was wrong. I told her that I was confident he was preaching from the Bible and what he was saying was absolute truth. I asked if she was born again, and she said no. I asked her why not, and she didn't know why. I asked if I could share something with her, and she excitedly said, "Sure!" I pulled a Gospel of John out of my pocket and shared Christ with her. I asked her to read it, and she said she would. I gave her my card and emphatically told her that if she had any questions, she should call me. She agreed. I guess I'll be going back to Buffalo Wild Wings again soon to follow up. Yesterday, I returned the rental car I had used over the weekend to travel to and from Pennsylvania. A young salesman named Matt drove me home from the enterprise agency. In the twenty minutes we rode together, the Lord opened the doors for a spiritual discussion. He had been in church his whole life until he went off to college. Then lost interest but still thought he was okay for all of eternity. I shared the Gospel in detail with him, and he was *very* concerned about going to hell. When we reached my home, I asked if I could pray for him, and he excitedly said yes. I put my hand on his shoulder and prayed for the Father to continue to draw Him and that he would give his life to Christ in repentance and faith. I reminded him that he had my number in their computer system and if he had questions he should call me. He said he would. Pray for Matt if this divine appointment comes to mind.

*****

Last night on the way to Hershey, we stopped for dinner. Our waitress's name was Katie. I told her that we always asked a blessing on our meals, and we always pray for our server. I asked how we could pray for her. She was quite stunned and then said I was going to make her cry. I said, "Please don't cry." Too late. She burst into tears. She calmed down and asked me to pray for her family. I asked if there was someone in particular who needed prayer, and she told me her dad did. I asked for his name and told her we'd pray for her and her dad. She thanked us and left. We left her a Gospel of John with a personal note in the front and a great tip. Now it's up to our Lord.

*****

Today I was filling in on a vacant bus run for the school district. After the preride checklist, a lady came to the door of the school bus and introduced herself as Jean. She was assigned to ride with me this morning to check out the route. The management was hoping she would take the morning and afternoon run going forward. In the course of conversation, I found out the she has never been to church but always felt there is a God. I had the opportunity to go through the Way of the Master questions with her and share the *One Second After You... Die* booklet with her. There was also an opportunity to pray for her as she had a cancerous tumor in her breast fifteen years ago, which required a lumpectomy, and another one has recently appeared that needs to be looked at. Jean thanked me for the book and said she would read it. She may ride again with me tomorrow, so I'll be able to follow up.

*****

I went trick or treating with my son and his family last night. We stopped at a house that he might be interested in buying. I saw a Virginia Game Commission truck in the driveway, and my son told me that one of them works for the Game Commission. As we walked up to the house, the husband and wife were outside waiting for the kids to stop by. I was wearing my Pennsylvania Game Commission Deputy Jacket, and I introduced myself. We met Jamie and Jade; and I found out that it was Jamie, the wife, who worked for the Game Commission. She is the bear biologist for the state... How cool. We swapped a bunch of stories and talked for quite a while, while my son and his family continued on their trick or treating route. They eventually returned for me, and we went back to their house. Sadly, I was so engrossed in the conversation that I neglected to share the Gospel with them... *And* I had Gospel literature in my pocket for just such an occasion! Fail! That night, I felt conviction as I realized that I never told them about Jesus.

So today after church, I told my son I had to stop at their house and complete my ambassadorship assignment before heading home. When I got to their house, Jamie was outside, and I got to share my faith with her. I gave her a camo-covered Gospel of John and a *One Second After You... Die* booklet to read. I included my card and told her to call if she had any questions after reading what I gave her. Now it's up to the Father!

*****

Last night, I went to dinner with my son and his family. He picked a *really* good barbeque restaurant near his home, and we got a waitress named Savanna to serve us. I asked how we could pray for her, and she immediately squatted down and told me about her brother Sean, who had done two tours as a marine sniper in Afghanistan and was shot in the stomach. He recovered from the wound but was given a medical discharge as he was unable to continue as a combat marine. He was offered a desk job, but Sean desperately wanted to be back in Afghanistan with his brothers in arms. So Sean declined the position and has been suffering from PTSD and began drinking.

He is thirty years old and struggling. We agreed to pray for him, and after praying, the thought popped into my head that I should connect my good friend Charlie (retired first sergeant from the corps) and Sean. I was convinced that Charlie could help him, even if it was just via telephone. Charlie agreed to speak with him. I got Sean's number from Savannah and gave her a Gospel of John with a nice note written in the front. And it just so happened that I also had a camo-covered Gospel of John with me. I wrote a note to Sean telling him I'd be praying for him and gave him Charlie's info so they could connect. Pray that the Lord will use Charlie to help this young marine find eternal peace with a new relationship with Jesus Christ and that his life will get on track.

*****

I have been trying to sell two Harley-Davidson saddlebag liners on Craigslist, and I received a call from a man named Dan, who lives about two miles east of me. We scheduled a time for him to come and look at the saddlebag liners. When he arrived, we had a long conversation about my Indian, and he showed me photos of the Harley he had customized. In the course of conversation, I found out that he knows my son-in-law's dad (Paul) very well; and in fact, my son-in-law, granddaughter, and Paul have hunted behind Dan's uncle Dave's property for many years. In fact, I even went with my son-in-law to help him build a blind in the woods behind Dave's place several years ago. As the conversation continued, Dan put two and two together and said that his daughter Taylor and my granddaughter Maya were best friends several years ago. As it turns out, I know his daughter Taylor! So we reminisced about things they had done together, and I had the opportunity to share Christ with Dan. I gave him a Gospel of John to take home and read and he agreed to do that. I pray the Lord will use our time together and the truth of His Word to save Dan and his family. Small world, huh?

*****

A local school district called and asked me to drive this Thursday and Friday mornings for a driver taking a couple of days off. So I would know the route, I was asked to ride with the driver this morning. His name is Steve. As I began the route, I quickly realized that I had already filled in on this route last month. Between runs, Steve would park at a local grocery store parking lot and chat with another driver. In the course of conversation, they asked why I don't drive mornings and afternoons, and I told them that I have a ministry and have to work on that most of the day. They asked what I did, and I explained what I teach. We then completed the second part of the run, and as we were returning to the transportation garage, I asked him if he went to church. He said he had been going to the church in Hamburg all of his life and sang in the choir. I asked if his church preached on the plan of salvation. He said, "I don't know." Hmmm… I asked if he was born again, and he didn't know. I explained the Gospel to him and asked if I could give him something to read. I gave him two copies of *One Second After You… Die* and asked if he would read it and give the other one to his friend when they meet at the grocery store. He agreed.

Had the transportation coordinator remembered that I had already done that route, I wouldn't have had to come in today, and I wouldn't have even met Steve and the other bus driver. Praise the Lord for His sovereignty and for this divine appointment today. I am adding both drivers to my daily prayer list for salvation.

God at Work in Williamsport, Pennsylvania

Yesterday I was returning from speaking at Lamoka Baptist Camp's "Teen No Retreat" and stopped for dinner in Williamsport. This is a regular place for us to stop and have dinner when we are traveling through the area, so I know the manager and many of the waitresses by name. Over the years, I have shared the Gospel with many of the ladies and left them Gospel literature and a great tip. Yesterday, I had a waitress I had never seen before. Her name was Lisa. I asked if she was new, and she said she had been working some day shifts there as the hostess for the past year and tended bar at night someplace else. The management asked her if she'd consider being a server, and she agreed to do it every other Saturday. Yesterday was her first day in this position.

As I finished dinner and was waiting for the check, another waitress whom we have known since 1989 saw me and came over to the table to say hi and catch up. Her name is Rhonda. She was so excited and asked me if I remembered giving another waitress named Marcy a *One Second After You... Die* booklet some time ago. I said I did remember, and at that time, I also got a chance to share the Gospel with the manager, Fred, and gave him the same booklet. Rhonda told me that Marcy read the booklet and God was working in her heart. She knew that Rhonda was a believer and was asking her all kinds of spiritual questions. Rhonda said that "Marcy is really seeking God." She added that Marcy has come to church with Rhonda for the past three weeks! PTL! I also found out that Rhonda's father is a Baptist minister. Why that didn't come up in conversation over the years, I don't know; but I gave her my card and asked her to speak with her dad about what I do and to check out my website. She agreed. Lord willing, I'll be sharing the MAD Live Event in that church at some point. Please pray for Marcy's conversion.

*****

I was at the gas pump this morning, and a man on the other side of the pump watched me pull up on the Indian. As I was filling my tank, he started a conversation about the bike, engines, and the negative effects of ethanol on engines. We ended up in a spiritual discussion, and I got to share Christ with Dick.

*****

This evening, I officiated a high school boys' varsity soccer scrimmage. When we met the coach of the visiting team before the game, he mentioned that his wife was having brain surgery for cancer. The Holy Spirit worked on me during the game and impressed on me to pray with him for his wife. So after the game and the hand-shakes, I told him that God was telling me to pray for his wife. He got very excited and said they could use all the prayers they could get. I asked what her name was, laid my hand on his shoulder, and prayed for the Lord to heal Judy or to use the doctors to heal her. I prayed for wisdom, skill, and guidance for the doctor, and for peace and quick healing for Judy, her husband and the family. He thanked me over and over again, and we talked some more. Please keep Judy in your prayers as the Lord brings this story to mind. Thanks.

*****

I was reading my Bible this morning when I heard a repetitive thumping sound coming up the road. I glanced out the window and saw a car with both passenger side tires flat driving up the road. I thought he won't be going too far like that.

Several hours later, I went out to speak with farmers to try to find a place to archery hunt. As I went up the road, I saw the same vehicle facing the opposite direction on my street with two people trying to pump up the flat tires. As I had an air compressor in the back of my truck, I pulled over, got out, opened the tailgate of my truck, and pulled the air hose out. I filled the rear tire for them and ran out of air in the compressor, as I hadn't filled it in some time. So I told them I'd be right back, turned my truck around, and headed back down the street to my house. I connected an extension cord to the compressor, refilled it, and headed back up to the stranded father and son. I filled the front tire and made sure the back one was full as well. They thanked me profusely and wanted to know if they could buy me some beer to pay me back. I thanked them and said that wouldn't be necessary and that I had something for them. The looked at each other kind of puzzled; and I reached into the truck, pulled out a Gospel of John with the plan of salvation in it and a *One Second After You... Die* booklet. I gave the Gospel to the young man and the other booklet to his dad. I explained what was in the book and how it could impact where they'd spend eternity. They thanked me for it, and I went on with my business. PTL!

Five Divine Appointments Today

As I went to leave the hotel this morning at 7:00 a.m., I went to the front office and rang the bell so they would open the door. An Indian lady came and let me in, and I noticed a large Buddha statue on the counter of the front desk. I checked out and asked if I could share something with her as someone just got in line behind me. She said, "Sure." I pulled out a *One Second After You... Die* booklet, explained what it was, and gave it to her to read. She seemed very grateful and said she would read it.

I then found a place to eat breakfast and got a server named Jonathan. I asked how I could pray for him, and he gave me a very general half-hearted request. I pressed him a little for something more specific and important to him, and he opened up and asked me to pray for his dad, Vincent, who was having some kind of an issue with his brain. Doctors were trying to figure how to treat the problem. I agreed to pray for him; and Jonathan put his hand on my shoulder, squeezed it, and said, "Thank you so much!"

I drove to the church and saw a Lobster Pound Restaurant on the way. Lobster was what I really wanted for dinner; I made up my mind to stop there after the training. I set up for the MAD Live Event and equipped twenty more people today. After I finished, I was loading the car in the ninety-degree plus heat and was quite sweaty. I decided to change my dress shirt before leaving. I picked out a Lancaster County Choppers T-shirt and put it on. I drove to the Lobster Pound Restaurant at about 3:20 p.m.—a little early for dinner but tough... I'm eating now.

I went into the restaurant, and a waitress named Oanna from Rumania selected a table for me to sit at. There was only one couple in the restaurant, and they were on the other side of the room. As I sat down, the man saw my shirt and asked me if I was from Lancaster County, Pennsylvania. I told him, "No. I'm from Berks County." He said he was from Lancaster County, and I inquired where. He replied, "Strasburg." I told him I knew where that was and asked if he was on vacation. They replied, "Yes, how about you?" I told them I was on the Cape to teach lifestyle evangelism. The conversation continued across the restaurant, and there was a lot of "spiritual" content. He asked me how I got into doing what I do, and I mentioned my police and computer background, and he lit up. He and his family have been manufacturing body armor, ballistic shields, holsters, and other police gear for years. We talked about police work, and his wife commented about the variety of things I had done in my life. I finally asked where they went to church, and they told me that they don't go to church, but the lady was raised Presbyterian, and he was raised Methodist. They also had some Catholic in their family. So I asked where he thought he would go if he died to today, and he said, "Heaven." I asked him if he was sure of that, and he said that there are many interpretations of the Bible, and he believed that he would go to heaven because he has always lived his life according to the Ten Commandments. Bingo! So I asked him how he was doing with that. He said he was doing well, and I asked if I could put that to the test. He agreed. So we did the Way of the Master thing, and he recognized that he had broken every one of the Commandments. I explained that this is the reason that God sent His Son to die on the cross for our sins. If they surrendered their lives to the Lordship of Christ in repentance and faith, a supernatural thing will happen to them, and they'd be born again. They were closing out their check, and I asked if I could get them something to read from the car. The agreed. I brought them a business card and a *One Second After You... Die* booklet, explained the content, and told them to call me if they had questions. He said, "Yeah, you're right up the road. We could get together for dinner and talk sometime." I agreed.

Then I had a long conversation with Oanna and was able to share Christ with her as well, and of course, I left a great tip.

What a day... Five divine appointments, and two of them would never have happened if I hadn't put that particular shirt on and stopped at the restaurant at that time. God is amazing, PTL!

*****

I am on Cape Cod for a MAD Live Event tomorrow. The pastor of the church I'll be teaching in recommended a casual seafood restaurant for me to have dinner at. I went to the restaurant; and the way it's set up—you order at a counter and pay for your food, and they call your number when the order is up and ready. The main part of the restaurant had someone seated at every table. There's a door on a narrow side hallway that allows people parked behind the restaurant to park in the rear and enter the facility. In that narrow hallway were two tables for two. No one was seated there, so I took the table closest to the main dining area of the restaurant and waited for my number to be called. An older lady sat at the other table for two, and she asked me to keep an eye on her two grandchildren (ages eight and nine), who insisted they could get all of the food by themselves. I keep an eye on them and updated her as their orders were coming out. She asked me if I was from the area, and I told her I was from Pennsylvania. She asked if I was on vacation, and I told her that I was on the Cape to teach tomorrow. She asked me what I teach...open door! I got up and went over to her table and explained what I would be teaching and gave her the Gospel of John that I had in my packet. This woman was *so* grateful for me sharing it with her, and I included my phone number if she had questions. She repeatedly thanked me for sharing it with her and told me she'd think about what I shared. She was truly excited! PTL!

I'm not born again... I'm a Baptist.

Tonight, we went out to dinner with our son, daughter-in-law, and two grandkids. We had a short wait for a table, so my family sat on the benches in the lobby of the restaurant. I sat on one by myself as the other benches were now full. A lady came in with her adult daughter and granddaughter. They were told they'd have a very short wait. They walked over to the bench I was sitting on, and I stood up and offered them my seat. The older said, "Thank you, but if I sit down, I won't be able to get back up." I smiled and said I'd be glad to help her get up. She smiled, thanked me, and sat down. A few minutes later, the hostess called their name, and as I was standing next to the bench, I reached out, and she grasped my hand, and I pulled her to her feet. She thanked me, and I told her to yell when she wanted to leave the restaurant, and I'd come help her get up (with a smile). She laughed and went with the hostess.

As I sat across the restaurant from her, I felt like I needed to share Christ with her. So I got up and went across the restaurant to find them. She saw me coming and smiled. I asked if she had a whistle to blow to get my attention when she wanted to leave. She laughed. I introduced myself and asked if I could share something with her. She said that would be fine. I asked her what she believed spiritually, and she told me she was a Baptist. I asked her if she was born again, and she said, "No. I am a Baptist!" I handed her a *One Second After You...Die* booklet and told her she needed to be a born-again Baptist. I then explained what the booklet was about and offered it to her as a gift if she would read it. She said she definitely would read it, and I told her it was nice meeting her and went back to my table.

"I'm not born again... I am a Baptist." Priceless!

*****

I just went to the Redner's Grocery Store to pick up a couple of items. I normally go the self-checkout, but I felt like I needed to go to this one particular line where there was a live cashier. When the total came up and the cashier saw that my change was $6.66, she freaked out! Her hands started shaking, and she tried several time to reach into the drawer to get my change, and she finally apologized and said she was giving me $6.70 change because she was very superstitious and didn't want to count out $6.66. I told her that there was no reason to be fearful of that number. She wasn't convinced. Unfortunately, my Gospel literature was in the car...not with me... Fail! So I went out to the car and returned to the store. She was speaking with the front-end manager when I approached her, and she smiled when she saw me. I told her why she didn't need to be fearful of that number and gave her a *One Second After You... Die* booklet to read. I told her if she took to heart what's in that booklet, she would never have to be fearful again. She smiled and repeatedly said, "Thank you!" as she clutched the booklet. As I was leaving, she was sharing with the manager what had happened.

*****

Last night, Cathy and I went out to try an Italian restaurant that had been recommended to us. We had a waitress named Chanita. I offered to pray for her, and she gave me a request. We prayed for her request, and a short time later, she came back to the table and told us that she was very touched by what we did for her. In all the years of being a waitress, no one had ever offered to pray for her. We ended up sharing the Gospel with her and leaving a *One Second After You… Die* booklet and a great tip.

I rode with another driver whose name is Kwan. I was going to be doing his morning run while he was having some test done prior to back surgery. I asked him if I could pray for him. He agreed, so I laid hands on him and prayed for his healing and salvation.

*****

Yesterday I spoke with Maran, the Indian man I shared Christ with a couple of weeks ago. He read *One Second After You… Die* and asked for more to read. I gave him a Gospel of John and invited him to church. He said "not this weekend," so I will try again. When I left, he was in the driver's room reading the plan of salvation in the front of the Gospel.

Today I did a MAD Live Event in Valley View, Pennsylvania. We had just over twenty people attend. I praise the Lord that two of the people left the training with a new eternal home in heaven. As I left, a lady was walking a cute little dog that looked a little like our dog. I stopped in the middle of the road and spoke with her about her dog. I showed her a pic of Buddy and asked if I could share something with her. She said yes. I pulled out a *One Second After You… Die* booklet and explained what it was, and she cheerfully took it saying she would definitely read it. She thanked me, and I drove home. God is good!

*****

I was riding with a bus driver named Wendy today, learning her route. We had a layover between school runs and had a nice conversation. The Lord opened the door for me to share my story and the plan of salvation with her. She has virtually no church background although she went to church when she was a little girl. She was going to the hospital today for a second mammogram because the first one she had showed some areas of concern. I asked if I could pray for her before we finished at the transportation lot, and she agreed. So I prayed for her healing and her salvation and gave her a *One Second After You... Die* booklet to read. We will discuss it next week. Praise the Lord!

*****

Divine Surprise

Tonight, I went to a local sub shop to get a sandwich for dinner. It is called the Steak Shack, and it is located in a shopping center parking lot not far from home (great cheesesteaks!). There was an older lady who arrived just before me. She placed her order at the drive-up window, pulled around the building, and parked, waiting for her order to be ready. I placed my order at the drive-up window and pulled around the building, parking next to her. A short time later, I looked in my rearview mirror, and the lady in the sub shop was waving attempting to get the attention of the lady parked next to me. I called out to her to let her know her sandwich was ready. She attempted to start her car, and it wouldn't start. I went over to see if I could help, and her battery was definitely dead. I asked her where she lived, and she told me Wernersville on Hill Road where the older folks' home was. I told her that I lived not far from there and, if she wanted, I would be happy to drive her home. She thanked me and said she had AAA, and she would eat her sandwich in the car and wait for them. I asked if I could share something with her, and she said, "Sure!" I pulled out a *One Second After You... Die* booklet and began to explain the plan of salvation to her. She stopped me and said that it wasn't necessary as she had already been born again. I asked her what church she went to, and she told me, "Glad Tidings." I told her that I had spoken there before, and she said, "Yes. You're Don Sunshine." Wow. That was a surprise. I asked if she needed anything else, and she assured me she was fine, so I left. Small world.

*****

Today we had to run an errand, and Cathy suggested having breakfast out. We stopped at a local iHop and had a server from India named Raja. I did our normal routine and told him that we always asked God to bless our meal, and we always prayed for our server. God had chosen him to be our server, and I asked how we could pray for him today. He gave me a simple request, and Cathy and I asked God to bless our meal, and we brought Raja's request before the Lord. We also asked the Lord to use the literature we'd be leaving to draw Raja to Himself and that he'd be saved.

A short time later, Raja returned to our table and asked me why I offered to pray for him. I explained that we do it every time we go out to eat. I asked him what he believed, and he gave me a very general philosophical answer. I asked him what the source of his beliefs were and how did he know his source(s) were true. He didn't have a good answer for that but said it was a "feeling" that he had having been born and raised in India with so many different religions to be exposed to. I simply shared the Gospel with him and told him that I was leaving him a Gospel of John to read. I then gave him a *One Second After You... Die* booklet, and explained what is in it. He thanked me for it and put it in his apron. I told him that my contact info was in the Gospel and if he had any questions to please call me. He said he would. PTL!

*****

I was away ministering on Friday night, Saturday, and all day Sunday. Cathy did not come with me on this trip. So I returned home on Sunday evening, and we decided to go out and have dinner together. We went to a local restaurant and had a server by the name of John. I asked John how I could pray for him as we are going to be asking a blessing on our meal before we ate. John jokingly said he wanted big tips for the night. I laughed and said, "Seriously, how can we pray for you?" He then told me that his brother had a very successful auto repair business in the city of Reading. He was expanding, and John was going to be going to work with him in the new location. John said he would be graduating from Kutztown University next month and they would be opening the new business. He would be giving up this serving job at that time. I thanked him for giving me something to pray about, and he left the table. After our meal was over, John approached our table and asked, "So tell me the words you used to pray for me." (This has never happened to us before.) I told him that we asked God to bless him in his new business and that they would have much success and happiness doing it together. I then added that I also prayed that John would read the Gospel of John that I would be leaving for him. I picked it up and showed it to him. I opened it up, and I said that I prayed that God would use this Gospel of John and the truth contained in it to draw you to Himself for salvation. John then squeezed into the booth and sat next to me, and we were sitting hip to hip. I slid over to make room, and he said, "Tell me more." So I asked him if he attended church. A little smirk appeared on corner of his mouth and quickly went away. I laughed and said, "Are you going to lie to me?" He laughed and said no. He said he hadn't been to church in quite a while and that he was raised Catholic. I told him I was raised Catholic also. I then told him that God was not interested in religion. He wants each of us to have a personal relationship with us through His Son. After explaining the plan of salvation to him, I told him to please call me anytime, day or night, if he had questions about what he read. He assured me that he would. Cathy and I left rejoicing in this amazing divine appointment and pray that God will save our new friend John.

The Verizon Guy

We changed services, switching our TV, Internet, and phone. The Verizon guy (Jay) came today to do the Internet and phone. He was a really nice guy, and he is very into motorcycles... Hmmm... divine appointment? He owns two Harleys, and we had a great time talking about motorcycles and riding. I had the opportunity to share the Gospel with him and gave him one of Mark Cahill's booklets entitled *One Second After You... Die.* I also gave him some delicious venison meat sticks as a snack and wished him s Merry Christmas. God is good.

Mike at Applebees

We were supposed to go to Texas Roadhouse for my birthday. I like to go early to beat the crowds (I don't like to sit and wait at a restaurant). Even though we got there early, it was packed with about a half-hour wait. So Cathy and I went to plan B (Applebees). It was just a few miles down the road, and there was no wait. Our server was named Mike, and we got to pray for him and share the Gospel. Now it's up to the Lord to do His thing.

*****

I went to the chiropractor today. It is a forty-three-mile ride each way, and I knew I would not be able to make it on the amount of gas that I had in the car. Sure enough, on my way home, the warning light came on, and I decided to stop at the Love's Truck Stop in Shartlesville as the gas is less expensive there that where I live. This is a very large station, and almost all of the pumps were not being used. I selected a place to stop and began refueling my car. The windows of the car were covered with salt, so I decided to clean them with the station supplied squeegee. A car pulled in and stopped to the right of my car, and I noticed the car had New Jersey plates on it. As I walked around to the rear of my car to clean the rear window, the lady from

New Jersey said, "Excuse me…is your windshield washer freezing?" I said no, and we began to discuss what might be causing hers to freeze up. She retrieved a gallon of windshield washer fluid from the rear of her car and showed it to me. It was good to thirty below zero. She sprinkled it on her windshield and turned her wipers on the clean the windshield. She then said that she didn't have the time to keep stopping on her way home. I asked her where she lived in New Jersey, and she said, "Hoboken." We talked about New Jersey a little, and I asked where she was coming from. She said she was visiting her sister, and then she started to cry. I asked her what was wrong, and she said her sister was dying of cancer. I told her how sorry I was and asked if I could pray for her and her sister. She said, "Yes!" I asked her name and what her sister's name was. She said her sister's name was Suzie and her name was Sissy. I put my hand on her shoulder, and she said, "Before you pray, please remember to pray that my windshield washer wouldn't freeze and that I will get home safely." I agreed. I prayed for both of them and went into my car to get a Gospel of John to share with her, and I was out! But God, in His providence, made sure there was a Mark Cahill booklet entitled *One Second After You… Die* in the console. How appropriate for this situation! I asked if I could share it with her and explained it to her. She agreed she would read it, and I told her to be sure to share it with her sister ASAP. She agreed to do that and thanked me many times as we headed our separate ways. Isn't God good? Look at all of the things that had to happen in His perfect timing for us to meet at that time and place so I could invite them to go to heaven when they die.

Divine Appointment

We have a Bose Acoustic Wave Sound System that never gets used, so I decided to sell it on Craig's List. I got a response from a man name John who said he wanted to come and buy it. I knew the meeting was more than just about selling a radio. It was a divine appointment. John showed up this morning and bought the radio. I shared one of Mark Cahill's booklets entitled, "1 Second After you…

die" with him. He said he appreciated what I shared but that he was LDS. We talked a little more and I told him I would send him a video that he should watch and an incredible oatmeal recipe from our friends Bruce and Kim in Florida. I did that. Now it's in the hands of our Lord!

Divine Appointment in Maryland

Divine appointment—I was passing through Maryland today and stopped at Chick-fil-A for a drink. As I was leaving the parking lot, a lady flagged me down. She was pregnant and had no coat on in the ten-degree weather. She asked me if I would jump start her car, and she said had cables. So I pulled my rental up next to her car and told her to sit in her car out of the wind. I asked her why she had no coat on, and she said she left it at home. I kidded her that her mother would not be happy if she knew her daughter was out in this weather without a coat. After a few attempts, the car started. I had her turn on her heat and roll the window down, and I shared Christ with her. I gave her a Gospel of John from the PTL, and she kept thanking me over and over for stopping and helping her. All glory to God!

Very Cool Divine Appointment

Divine appointment—I went to the chiropractor today. It is a forty-three-mile ride each way, and I knew I would not be able to make it on the amount of gas that I had in the car. Sure enough, on my way home, the warning light came on, and I decided to stop at the Love's Truck Stop in Shartlesville as the gas is less expensive there that where I live. This is a very large station, and almost all of the pumps were not being used. I selected a place to stop and began refueling my car. The windows of the car were covered with salt, so I decided to clean them with the station supplied squeegee. A car pulled in and stopped to the right of my car, and I noticed the car had New Jersey plates on it. As I walked around to the rear of my car to clean the rear window, the lady from New Jersey said, "Excuse me…is your windshield washer freezing?" I said no, and we began to discuss what might be causing hers to freeze up. She retrieved a gallon of windshield washer fluid from the rear of her car and showed it to me. It was good to thirty below zero. She sprinkled it on her windshield and turned her wipers on the clean the windshield. She then said that she didn't have the time to keep stopping on her way home. I asked her where she lived in New Jersey, and she said, "Hoboken." We talked about New Jersey a little, and I asked where she was coming from. She said she was visiting her sister, and then she started to cry. I asked her what was wrong, and she said her sister was dying of cancer. I told her how sorry I was and asked if I could pray for her and her sister. She said, "Yes!" I asked her name and what her sister's name was. She said her sister's name was Suzie and her name was Sissy. I put my hand on her shoulder, and she said, "Before you pray, please remember to pray that my windshield washer wouldn't freeze and that I will get home safely." I agreed. I prayed for both of them and went into my car to get a Gospel of John to share with her, and I was out! But God, in His providence, made sure there was a Mark Cahill booklet entitled *One Second After You… Die* in the console. How appropriate for this situation! I asked if I could share it with her and explained it to her. She agreed she would read it, and I told her to be sure to share it with her sister ASAP. She agreed to do that and thanked me many times as we headed our separate ways. Isn't God good? Look at all of the things that had to happen in His perfect timing for us to meet at that time and place so I could invite them to go to heaven when they die.

Incredible Divine Appointment Today at the Chiropractor

Amazing diving appointment—I went to the chiropractor this morning to have him work on my neck. When I arrived, the two treatment rooms were full, and there were four others in the waiting room waiting for their turn. This has never happened before. So I figured it was going to take a while for me to get into the treatment room. I waited about fifteen minutes and then decided to save a little bit of time by making my next appointment before the treatment, rather than after. As we discussed the few open dates early next week, due to cancellations this week in advance of the Nor'easter coming, a man in ski bibs came in and stood at the receptionist's counter near me. Rachel, the receptionist, asked me why I couldn't come later next week, and I told her I'd be on a ministry trip to Florida, doing about 3,500 miles…2,500 of them on a motorcycle. I finished my conversation with her, and the man who came in then said, "I need help… I am lost." (Can you say open door?) Rachel asked where he was trying to go, and he was from out of the area and was trying to find the Blue Mountain Ski Resort. I told him he was way too far west of Allentown, and I didn't know the best way to get there from New Tripoli, unless he went way out the way. I suggested Rachel MapQuest it for him, and as she was doing that, he said, "So what do you ride?" We ended up having a fifteen- to twenty-minute motorcycle discussion in the office, and as he went to leave, I told him I'd like to invite him to come on our Smoky Mountains Motorcycle Adventure in May. He said he was interested, so I walked him out and grabbed a ministry business card from my truck for him. I also picked up one of Mark Cahill's booklets entitled *One Second After You… Die*. I asked if I could share this with him, and he listened as I explained what the booklet was and what the truth in it could do for his eternity. We ended up in a forty-five-minute Gospel presentation and Q&A session in the parking lot. His name is Bob, and there's a lot more to the conversation, but I don't have time to go into all of the details. I said to him, "Bob, I believe with all of my heart that God arranged for you to miss the ski resort and end up forty minutes away at this doctor's office to meet me so I could invite you to go to heaven when you die." He said, "That thought has already crossed my mind." I asked him if we could connect sometime soon and that I'd like to start a friendship with him. He said he'd like that and would contact me after he got home." Bob is sixty-three years old, and I ask that you pray for him. Isn't God amazing? Look at all of the things that had to take place for me to meet this man. And his heart was wide open. The seed has been planted. Now it is up to God to cause the growth.

I went back into the office and apologized to Rachel. I said, "I am sorry I missed the appointment, but that man needed to hear about Jesus." She said it was okay but that I had to wait another forty-five minutes if I was going to see the doctor. I told her I couldn't because I had a lunch appointment with a young man I am discipling and mentoring. But that's okay, because the diving appointment trumps the chiropractic appointment any day of the week.

MAD Live Event and First Divine Appointment

This was to be posted on Saturday night. However, we had no Wi-Fi, so it is being posted one day late.

We completed the MAD Live Event today in Pinellas Park. We praise God for four people surrendering their lives to Christ in repentance and faith. We want to thank Bob and Esther for being amazingly gracious hosts for Ron and me while we were in the St. Pete area.

We then headed 105 miles north to Leesburg to spend the night and next day with our dear friends from New Jersey, Paul and Ellen. They winter in Leesburg. As we sped along (at the speed limit of seventy miles per hour), I changed lanes on the bike and immediately realized there was a two-by-four-by-eight lying across my lane. I have never hit a two-by-four on a motorcycle at seventy miles per hour before, but thankfully, I got over it without incident. Ron then hit it as well without issue.

On the way, we stopped for a bathroom break, and God provided our first divine appointment of the trip. We parked the bikes outside the rest area building, and a female employee walked up and was picking up pieces of trash around our bikes. As she approached my bike, I commented on how hot it was to be doing that job in the parking lot. She said she prefers to do it after dark as it is cooler. I commented that it's pretty hot with an engine between our legs. She agreed that it would be hotter on the bikes than in the parking lot. I got off my bike, grabbed a Gospel of John, and headed over to speak with her. I asked her what her name was, and she said, "Molly." I told her my name and asked if I could share something with her. She said, "Sure!" I shared my faith in Christ with her and explained that the book I was giving her was a Gospel of John with the plan of salvation outlined in the front. I offered it to her as a gift and asked if she would read it. She agreed to read it and share it with her son, and she thanked me for it. We arrived at Paul and Ellen's safely and enjoyed dinner with them. We'll be going to church with them tomorrow.

Trip Update and Divine Appointments

We rode 275 miles today to Key West. The weather was good and *hot*. We had some adventures on the road when we got onto the Florida Turnpike, and it required a Sun Pass, and we didn't have one. Long story, but we got it all straightened out.

We stopped or breakfast at an iHop at 10:00 a.m. and had a waiter named Mo. His wife had just passed away, and he was working as a Denny's manager and waiting tables to pay for her bills. We prayed for him and shared a Gospel of John with him.

We crossed the seven-mile bridge where they filmed the movie, *True Lies*. We saw the part of the bridge where they landed the Harrier and the part of the bridge that they blew up with the missile. Pretty cool.

Pastor Chuck took us out to dinner, and we had a server named Rashad. We asked how we could pray for him, and he asked for prayer for the family of his twenty-two-year-old friend named Brian. He was walking along the sidewalk and tripped and fell, hitting his head. It killed him! We also got to share a Gospel with a young sailor from San Diego who was waiting in the restaurant with us before the meal.

We had a great time presenting part 1 of the MAD Live Event to a small group of people from the Eagles Rest Ministry. Part 2 is tomorrow night. We are blessed to be staying with a former pastor

Divine Appointments and 297 Safe Miles

Ron and I had got up this morning and were greeted by heavy rain. We packed the bikes and donned our rain gear for the ride back north. We met my old friend Craig Marston for breakfast, who opened the doors for us to minister in Key West. We then headed north on Route 1. As we approached the northern end of the Keys, the rain subsided, and we stopped for a caffeine beverage for Ron as he was very drowsy. Ron took the lead and was going to select a place to stop and get a drink. God did what God does, and after removing my rainsuit, a man came up to me and began asking questions about my trailer. We had a nice discussion, and I asked his name and where he was from. His name was Dave, and he was from Wall Township, New Jersey. I told him I was born and raised in New Jersey, and I then asked what he did for a living. He owns a bar and a business involving Border Collies being used to chase geese from runways and corporate lawns. The conversation continued, and it turns out that Verona Park (I was born and raised in Verona) is one of his clients. I asked if I could share something with him and shared the Gospel as well as one of Mark Cahill's little books—*One Second After You... Die.*

We parted ways, and Ron and I continued north to Jupiter. We stopped at the Harvest Bible Chapel and set up for tomorrow's MAD Live Event. We then headed to my friend Norm's to check on his son Ben. Ben had been surfing the day before, and after surfing, he was doing something in the water and got caught up in a Portuguese Man of War. He had burns and welts across his stomach and arm, and one tentacle somehow got in his mouth and onto his tongue. He was in pretty bad shape with a lot of toxins and ended up in the ER. He was home recovering, and we went to see him. Ben is on meds and is feeling better although the wounds itch like crazy. He said the pain was so bad he would much rather have broken a bone than be hit by one of them.

We then headed north toward Port St. Lucie to spend the night at our friends Bruce and Kim's home. On the way, we stopped for dinner and prayed for our waitress Amber, and we shared a Gospel of John with her. We are grateful to God for His protection on us for the 297 miles we did today.

A Very Cool Divine Appointment!

We completed the MAD Live Event at the Port St. Lucie Bible Church today, packed the bikes up, and prepared to head 155 miles north to Daytona. We stopped for dinner on the way and prayed for our waitress and her teenage daughters. We left her a Gospel of John with a nice note in it with a good tip.

As we left the restaurant, the temperature was dropping, so I thought it would be best to replace the mesh riding jacket I had been wearing with my leather one. That way I wouldn't have to stop and change as the temperature continued to drop. Ron kept his light-weight jacket on, and we continued north. After a while, my gas began to get low, and I thought we'd need to be stopping in the next twenty miles or so to refuel. Ron passed me and pulled in front of me as we traveled up Route 95. I followed him for a little while and then pulled out to pass him. As soon as I pulled out, he put his right turn signal on to exit, so I pulled in behind him. Ron got off the exit and pulled into a gas station. It was pretty empty except for a Mercedes parked on the side of the building. I began gassing my bike, and the man from the Mercedes came over to me and asked if I knew where the closest repair shop was. I asked him what the problem was, and he said he didn't know exactly, but he was overheating, and other things were not right. I said I would take a look at it and suspected he had a problem with his serpentine belt. I opened the hood of his car and shined my light behind the radiator, and the problem was obvious. His belt was shredded. I reached in and pulled out a handful of spaghetti like black shreds of his former serpentine belt and said, "Here's the problem." He wasn't going anywhere tonight. We discussed his options, and he said he was going to get a tow and get someone to drive him home 180 miles south. I detected a familiar New York accent and asked where he was from. "Brooklyn," he replied. I told him my dad was born and raised in Brooklyn. I asked what their names were, and he said Mike and Gina. I introduced Ron and myself and asked if I could share something with them, and he said, "Sure." I pulled out a Gospel of John and briefly explained what it was. He told me he was a Catholic, and I explained that I was, too, but that I had found the truth, briefly explaining the difference between religions and a relationship with God through His Son, Jesus Christ. I told him that I was sure that I was going to heaven when I died, and I wanted him and his wife to be there too. I then asked him if I could pray for them. They looked at each other and said yes. I put my hand on Mike's shoulder, and Ron put his hand on Gina's shoulder, and I prayed for them, thanking God for allowing us to meet them. I also said that even though this was an inconvenience for them, this was ordained of the Lord so we could meet them and share Christ with them. There was more content in the prayer, and when I concluded the prayer, Gina was in tears. She crossed herself and said, "Thank you," and walked back to her car. Mike also thanked me, and we walked away. I turned and saw Gina in the car, and I waved goodbye to her. She waved back. After we remounted the bikes and began to leave, I glanced back, and they were sitting on a picnic bench reading the Gospel of John! How cool is that! Praise God! This divine appointment made the perfect ending to our day. I can't wait to see whom we get to meet tomorrow!

Two Divine Appointments Each for Us So Far Today!

God's been busy! So far today, Ron and I have each had two divine appointments with people. I went out front to my motorcycle this morning, and a man rode a bicycle up to the house across the street. He had the highest ape hanger handlebars I had ever seen on a bicycle. He said, "Good morning," to me. I greeted him back and commented on the high-rise bars. He came over, and we talked. He is a carpenter named Fred, and he was working in the house across the street. We had a nice conversation, and I asked if I could share something with him. He said, "Sure!" I pulled one of the Gospels of John from my Tourpack and shared my faith with him. He said he would read it and thanked me for it.

This afternoon, we went to the Advance Auto sort to pick up two spark plugs for my bike. Ron and I each were met by a person in the parking lot and two thirty-minute conversations ensued. The man I met was named Rick Bush. He was sixty-two years old and has been sailing all around North and South America for the past seven years since he retired. He was a fascinating guy! I shared my faith with him and also gave him a Gospel of John to read. He said he would definitely read it because he had interest in spiritual things. We talked some more and bid him safe sailing and left. Can't wait to see who God has lined up for us next!

Best Day of Ministry Yet!

Ron and I woke up to some rain today. So we donned our rain gear and headed out to breakfast. We had a waitress named Becky, and we shared a Gospel of John with her and prayed for her and her mom, Kathy. We then went to Destination Daytona to check out the vendors. I saw the butt "Buffer Booth" and wanted to stop there and let Ron look at the gel pads to see if one of them could make him more comfortable on the long rides. In the course of conversation, it turns out that Pete lives in Ephrata, Pennsylvania...about twenty minutes from my house and Jim lives in Mechanicsburg, Pennsylvania. Jim is a Catholic, and Pete is an agnostic or atheist (he wasn't quite sure). I had a great conversation with each of them, sharing my testimony and the plan of salvation in detail. I gave Jim a Gospel of John, and I gave Pete the *One Second After You... Die* book.

We eventually ended up at the Cycle Gear store to help them move their inventory into a U-Haul truck to make room for the Bike

Night tonight. I had volunteered to help them when we were in the store yesterday. Ron and I cleared the showroom section ourselves… moving boxes of helmets, boots, bike covers, AVT jacks, and wheel chocks into the truck. Several of the store employees organized the goods in the back of the truck as we brought it in. When we were done, the manager, Mauro, and the four other employees were a little stunned that we came down to help expecting nothing in return. We just explained that we wanted to serve. I went to the back of the store to get my helmet and met Sal in the back room. If I judged by appearance, he would have been the least interested in what I had to share. Boy, would I have been wrong! He had tattoos all over and up his neck, and he was a pretty big dude. I started a conversation with him and gave a complete Gospel presentation and my testimony. He hung on every word and was shocked and very interested in the fact the he could know for sure where he was going to spend eternity. He seemed *very* concerned about his eternal destination. I shared the Gospel of John with him, and he saw the other book in my hand (*One Second After You… Die*) and asked if he could have that one as well. I said, "Sure," and gave him one. He said he would keep them with him and he would definitely read them today. We talked for a total of about ten minutes, and he asked if he could have my number if he had questions. Absolutely! He kept thanking me, and I hope to hear back from him. I then went to each of the other employees, Jim, Omar, Aaron, and Manager Mauro, and shared my testimony and the Gospel with them. Jim had some interest. Omar and Aaron not so much. When I finally got to Mauro, an Italian Catholic, he, too, hung on every word; and we never broke eye contact through the whole discussion. I gave him my phone number as well, and we'll see what the Lord does! What a day… Thank you, Jesus! April 4, 2014.

Divine Appointment with the Plumber

We had a plumber come in today to do some work for us. His name is Brian. I had a nice conversation with him for the three hours he was here. We talked about hunting and the Lord. Although he was raised in a Christian home and attended church when he was young, he led a rather rebellious life. Since getting married and having three sons, he got straightened out and got involved in hunting. That is his passion. He says he meets with God as the sun rises while he's in his tree stand. I explained that while that is a magical moment for sure. That would not get him into heaven. He agreed. I shared Mark Cahill's *One Second After You... Die* with him. He said he would read it and call me if he had questions. We'll see what the Lord does. He's a nice guy, and I'd love to see him in heaven someday.

Divine Appointment at the Drive-up Window

Today I had an open door to share Christ with the man who owns the Steak Shack in Sinking Spring. I spent about twenty minutes talking with him at his drive-up window about the Lord and then returned later for another twenty-minute conversation. When I returned the second time, he said that he couldn't think about anything but what I had shared with him on the first stop. I gave him something to read and included my phone number. I am hoping God will bless me with the privilege of leading him to true faith in Jesus Christ very soon.

*****

I've had a couple of great days of divine appointments. On Friday night, I was blessed to share Christ with our waitress Christina. This morning, I offered to pray for my server Chuck, at Cracker Barrel. He instantly welled up with tears and said I could pray for him as his dad had passed away this week. I prayed for him and his family. After breakfast, he came over, grabbed my hand, and thanked me profusely for paring for him. Tonight, I stopped at a restaurant that Pastor James had recommended, and I got a waitress named Tatiana. I ended up praying for her, and she came back to talk further. It is a *long* story, but we spent about ten minutes in a detailed Gospel discussion. I gave her a Gospel of John and a *One Second After You...*

Die booklet for her to read. She said she would contact me if she had any questions. It was awesome. Wish I could detail all of the cool stuff that happened.

*****

We decided to go out for a bite to eat for dinner tonight. We got a waitress named Kaila. I asked how I could pray for her, and she was totally taken by surprise. I asked her if anyone had ever offered to do that for her, and she said that she had been waitressing for seven years and no one had ever offered to pray for her. She thought for a second and asked me to pray for her family's health. I asked her if there was someone specifically she was thinking of who could use the prayers. She said her mom had just finished cancer treatments and she was hoping it wouldn't come back. I asked what her name was, and she replied, "Donna." I said we'd pray for her mom. She left our table, and after I prayed, I got up to go to the car for something, and Kaila was standing at the computer, and one of her coworkers was rubbing her on the back consoling her. Kaila was wiping tears from her eyes. I guess it really impacted her. She returned to our table time after time, giving us exceptional service, each time beaming with a smile on her face. We left the Gospel of John with a nice note in the front and a great tip. I pray the Lord uses the experience and the truth of His Word to rescue Kaila and her family for eternity.

*****

I met one of my neighbors when we moved in here two and a half years ago. His name is Dennis. I've seen him a couple of times since then and said hello. Yesterday I was blowing leaves off my front lawn, and he came outside to get into his truck. I shut the blower off and greeted him. When I asked how he was doing, he told me that he was heading to the doctor because he was in need of some additional back surgery. He told me that he was in a lot of pain. I went over to him and asked if I could pray for him. He said yes! So I laid my hand on his shoulder, and I prayed for his healing and for a reduction in the pain. He thanked me and got into his truck to head to the doctor. After finishing clearing my lawn, I noticed that his lawn had more leaves on it than mine did. So I went over and blew all of his leaves out into the street as well. Although it took me quite a while to clear his front lawn, he did not get home in time for me to see him again. So today I'm going to go over and to give him a copy of *One Second After You... Die* and share the Gospel with him.

*****

As usual, we planned on going down to Daytona Bike Week to share our faith with the people at the event. However, I made a huge mistake, and we were there a week early. No crowds, just vendors setting up. Ron and I met with vendors and offered to help them set up their displays. I spoke with Pete and Jim, vendors who sell the Butt Buffer gel seat implants. We spoke for about forty-five minutes as there were no customers to be had. Jim is a nonpracticing Catholic, and Pete is an atheist. I gave Jim a Gospel of John with the plan of salvation in it to read and shared a *One Second After You... Die* with Pete. It turned out that Pete is from Ephrata, Pennsylvania, about thirty minutes from where I live. He agreed to read the booklet, and we parted ways.

In April, I traded my H-D in on a new Indian with ABS. I wanted a butt buffer installed in this bike like I had on the H-D. I called Pete, made an appointment for yesterday, and drove down to meet him. As he was working on the seat, I revisited our previous spiritual conversation and asked if he had read the booklet. He had read it but wasn't convinced. We ended up in a sixty-five-minute conversation; and I told him about my best friend Chuck, who had been killed in a motorcycle accident in 2006 on a motorcycle that I had helped arrange for Chuck to buy. I shared Chuck's spiritual conversion with Pete and told him how much I still missed my best friend, mentioning that Chuck used to come down and hunt and always brought Maine lobsters for us to share. Pete then asked if I had ever seen an eighteen-pound lobster. Indeed I had at the lobster company on the wharf in Newport, Rhode Island. Pete told me that he caught one some time ago. This gave me a clue that Pete was a wreck diver, because that's about the only place you'll find a hundred-year-old lobster. I asked Pete if he was a wreck diver, and sure enough, he had been one. I mentioned that I used to wreck dive every summer out of Point Pleasant, New Jersey. He got a stunned look on his face and asked if I dove on the Sea Lion. Yep! That was the ship we chartered to wreck dive from! Pete said he was the first mate on the ship! We compared timelines, and sure enough, we had met over thirty years ago on the boat! I continued my spiritual conversation with him, and he was very open. I asked if he would listen to a set of six CDs by Chip Ingram called "Why I Believe." He said he would, so I ordered a set yesterday and will deliver them to him when they arrive. Can you see the hand of a sovereign God in all of this? What are the chances that all of these circumstances would happen to bring us together at this point in our lives? I added Pete to my daily prayer list, and I am trusting that all of this happened for a reason—so Pete would surrender his life to Christ in repentance and faith and be saved. I'll let you know what God does with Pete down the road.

*****

A local school district was desperate for bus drivers this week. They asked me if I could help them out and drive a bus route for them in the afternoon for a few days. After the first day on the bus, I could see that the road salt was excessively packed all over the bus, and the mirrors and windows were difficult to see out of and use. So the next day, I brought in some Windex and paper towels. I cleaned the windshield, side windows, and mirrors, and headed to the first school. As I drove up there, I realized that the mirrors still needed some work. I parked behind several other school district's vans which were parked in front of me in the school's driveway loop and got out to clean the mirrors again. As I finished the mirrors, I believe the Holy Spirit prompted me to clean the van windows and mirrors in front of me. I went to the van in front of me, sprayed Windex on the driver's outside mirror and window, and began cleaning them. The lady driving the van got this look of shock, amazement, and gratitude as I cleaned them for her. She smiled, rolled her window down, and thanked me profusely. Apparently, no one had ever done that for her before. I then cleaned the mirror and the window on the passenger side and proceeded to the van in front of her and did the same thing. I then had the opportunity to share a Gospel of John with the drivers.

*****

I had an ad on Craigslist to sell a treadmill. A man named Bob from Lebanon County called today and made an appointment to come and check out the treadmill. When he arrived, I showed him all the functions of the machine, and we ended up in a discussion about being in shape and staying in shape. I mentioned that winter is tough on me because I get inactive, but during the warmer weather, I referee high school soccer. The conversation continued, and it turns out that his son and my son played soccer together at East Stroudsburg University. His son was year behind mine. We shared some memories of games and events that occurred, and after loading the treadmill into his vehicle, I had the opportunity to share a Gospel of John with him and invite him to go to heaven when he dies. God is incredible…

Ron and I made it safely to West Columbia, South Carolina, in the truck. Seventy-nine degrees was the highest temperature we experienced on our way down in South Carolina (sorry for my friends up north!). Another divine appointment… I stopped at the Charlotte Indian dealer and met the service manager who recently moved down to North Carolina from Bally, Pennsylvania, near where I live! We also got to pray for our waitress Lynda tonight. The motorcycles and trailer are unloaded. We're organizing gear for tomorrow's four-hundred-plus-mile trip to Daytona Beach. Praying for warm, dry weather and safety for our trip and loads of divine appointments so we can share the love of Christ!

Very Cool Divine Appointment from Last Night

Last night, Cathy, Ron, and I went out for dinner before we left for South Carolina this morning. We had a server named Paul (not his real name). We offered to pray for him, and he gave us a request. He stayed and bowed his head while I prayed for him and his request. Today I received this e-mail from him:

> Hello, Don, this evening you guys came into Texas Roadhouse and I had the pleasure of serving you. I wanted to thank you for the book and the prayer. Also, I wanted to ask for your help. You asked if there's anything else that I needed prayer for and at first I could not think of anything to say. Then it hit me. What I always have been praying for myself, my girlfriend. I personally have grown up Christian and have had a strong relationship with God. I have been saved and could not be happier. A year ago I met my girlfriend who truly made me a better person. Her family is Catholic and they raised her Catholic but she no longer believes. It troubles me every day because I do not think she has been saved. She has such a loving heart but is hard headed when it comes to the things she believes in. She finds it hard that someone out there could "control her life." I always find myself praying for her and for strength to bring her to God but I really don't know what to do. Every time there is bad weather for example and she is driving I am scared that something bad could happen and ultimately I could never see her again. I guess what I am asking is for you to pray for her, and for me to have the strength to help her find God. I really appreciate the book, the prayer, and the tip tonight. I felt I had to reach

out to you once I started reading the book and I really want her to read it too. Thanks again!

I sent him a response to the e-mail and some additional info, and we hope to keep in touch.

Praise God for another opportunity!

Safely in Florida! Divine Appointments

We thank the Lord for safe travels to Florida. After close to four hundred miles, we are safely in Daytona Beach. The highest temperature that my info center thermometer registered was ninety-one degrees…yes, ninety-one. (Sorry.) As I was filling my tank in South Carolina, a lady started a conversation with me at the pump about Bike Week. Her name is Kim, and I shared the Gospel with her and gave her a Gospel of John to read. She was very grateful for it! We stopped again for gas after crossing into Florida. Ron was hungry, so we sat down in the convenience store/Subway. A man came up to me to talk about the Indian motorcycle. His name was Jonas, and he was from Ohio. His wife, Jeanie, had neck surgery in Florida three weeks ago, and they were slowly making their way home. In the course of conversation, I found out that he and his family are already followers of Jesus Christ and are involved in a Mennonite church at home. I asked Jeanie if I could pray for her, and we gathered in a small circle; and Ron prayed for her, the family, and their travels home. I gave Jonas my card and told him what I do. Maybe God will open the doors for me to go to his church to teach! The photo is my Indian loaded with all of our gear for the trip.

Friday's Events

Yesterday, we had the privilege of sharing Christ with our waitress at breakfast. As I sat outside putting on my rainsuit, a man named Brian approached me to talk about the Indian motorcycle.

It turns out that he works for Indian, and we had a nice discussion about the bikes and Bike Week. I ended up sharing a *One Second After You... Die* booklet with him and then realized I misplaced my phone. As I looked for the phone in the motorcycle, Ron continued the conversation with Brian. As I searched my saddlebags for the phone, another man approached me in the parking lot to talk about the Indian. As I turned the conversation to Christ, he professed his faith in the Lord, and we ended up in a nice time of fellowship.

We needed to stop at Cycle Gear so Ron Woudenberg could buy a new rain jacket, and we gassed the bikes up on the short ride to the store. Ron arrived a few minutes ahead of me, and as I approached the place where he was parked, I saw he was having a conversation with a man about the Victory motorcycle Ron was riding. I got off the bike, and Ron headed into the store. I continued the conversation with the man (named Bruce), and as I began to share the Gospel with him, he also indicated that he had been born again and attends a church not he beach every Sunday. He also told me that his wife and family were also followers of Jesus Christ. As the computers were "down" in the store and Ron was patiently waiting for them to come back "up," Bruce and I fellowshipped for some time. Ron finally gave up waiting on the computer, and we left for Jupiter.

On the way down, we met some good friends from previous trips, Bruce and Kim Herchenroder or lunch. We had some more fellowship over lunch and completed our trip to Jupiter.

Today we have a MAD Live Event in Jupiter, and then we'll be traveling north to Minneola for another MAD Live Event tomorrow. Continued prayers are appreciated as rain is expected today. Thank you!

Two More MAD Live Events Done!

I did my four MAD Live Event at the Calvary Church in Jupiter on Saturday. I was blessed by the folks who attended and had a chance to minister to. After completing the training in Jupiter, Florida, Ron and I headed north to Mineola. On the way, my Indian motorcycle had some error codes related to a clutch sensor. We stopped, and after restarting the motorcycle, they went away. We had some rain on the way up but not too much. We arrived safely in Minneola and met Pastor Bob. He took us out to dinner at Sonny's Barbecue, and we had a waitress named Jennifer. We offered to pray for Jennifer, and I filled out a Gospel of John with a personal note to her. I laid it on the bench next to me, and apparently, it's slipped between the bench and the wall, and I didn't realize it. So as we went to leave, I couldn't find the Gospel of John. I realized that it must've fallen between the bench and the wall. So I pulled out another Gospel of John and wrote her a second note. As we began to leave, Ron thought he could pull the booth away from the wall. He pulled it out, and I was able to retrieve the original Gospel of John. We joked that at our next restaurant, we would have to get a waitress named Jennifer so we could use the Gospel of John that we wrote Jennifer's name in. This morning, Pastor Bob came by and took us out to breakfast at the Cracker Barrel. As we entered, we were joking about asking for a waitress named Jennifer so we could share the already completed Gospel of John with her. As we walked up to the hostess station, guess what happened... The hostess's name was Jennifer! The three of us laughed in amazement, and I asked if she would be our waitress. She said no, because she would be serving as the hostess today. We ended up with the waitress named Cindy and were able to get a prayer request from her and pray for her. As we prayed, the Lord laid it on my heart to go up and share the Gospel of John with Jennifer, the hostess. I explained the situation to her, and she said, "Oh my, I was at church last night, and there are some things going on in my life, and I felt like I needed someone to pray for me, but I didn't ask anyone to pray for me. And now you came in and offered to pray for me!" We talked about her faith, and she professed to be born again. She asked me to pray for an unspoken request, which we did. We are both amazed at how God connected the two of us today.

We then traveled to Minneola to do a live event at the Alliance Church. At 9:40 a.m., while the leadership was praying for the event which started at ten, when an explosion occurred just outside the room we were in. It sounded like a transformer blew, and the lights went out. We opened our eyes and commented how that was not good. I thought that for the first time I would be doing the training without any audio or visual or PowerPoint. We finished praying, went outside, and the electric company had just arrived…that fast in a Sunday? He looked at the pole and said it was just a large fuse. He said he'd have it replaced in five minutes! At 10:03 a.m., the lights came back on! Wow! All praise to God that one teen gave his life to Christ at the training. Ron and I headed back to Daytona, stopped for dinner, and had a great conversation with a sister in the Lord and server at the restaurant name Kayle. She is a senior in high school. We had great conversation with her and prayed for her request. Then we completed our trip to Daytona. I am whipped and it is time for bed!

Thank You, Lord! What a Great Day!

What a great day we had! I was exhausted last night after the long day we had, and I was behind in my updates because the home we stayed in had no Wi-Fi. So I stayed up late to catch everyone up last night. I ended up "sleeping in" today until about 7:45 a.m.

After showers, Ron and I headed out to breakfast. We had a very nice lady named Faye as our server and were blessed to be able to pray for her needs and share the love of Christ with her.

We then went to the Speedway and test drove the Indian Roadmaster. What a nice bike! We saw Brian, with whom I shared a *One Second After You… Die* booklet yesterday, at the Indian demo ride area. I asked if he had read the booklet, and he said he had started it the night before but fell asleep in the middle of it as he, too, was exhausted. He said he would read it through.

We then walked over to where we thought the tram was running. We couldn't find it. I stopped to use the Porta-Jon (I know, TMI), and Ron said he was going over to check out the Moto Guzzi motorcycle display which was across the parking lot. I got out of the PJ and asked a passerby if he knew where the tram stop was. He told me he was looking for it too. We ended up in a nice conversation.

His name is Mike, and this was his first trip to Bike Week. He is from Minnesota but winters in central Florida. I ended up sharing the Gospel with Mike and giving him a Gospel of John to take and read. He gladly took it, and then I asked how I could pray for him. He asked me to pray for his daughter who was just diagnosed with Crohn's disease. I then walked over to meet Ron, and he was speaking with a sales guy named Shane. I got involved in some of the conversation and was able to share my hope story and the Gospel with him. I gave him a Gospel of John, and he said he would read it. We gave up on finding the tram and walked back to our bikes to ride them to the other side of the speedway to walk through the vendor area. We got there, and it was a zoo. I haven't seen the speedway this packed with people and motorcycles in years. I followed Ron who rode his bike through the crowds and into the vendor area. He stopped in front of a vendor and parked his bike, and I parked mine there as well. As I got off the bike, a man and a woman stopped to talk about the Indian I was riding. We had a nice conversation, and I eventually turned it to a spiritual one. I shared the Gospel with Bob and Stephanie, who hail from southeastern Ohio. I gave them a Gospel of John, which they said they would read.

We then stopped at the Allstate Insurance booth and entered a free drawing for a chance to win a custom motorcycle. The ladies who take your info are employees of a marketing firm hire by Allstate to do this at Bike Week. After giving Jackie my info, I shared the Gospel with her and gave her a Gospel of John to read.

We went to dinner and had a waitress named Teri. We offered to pray for her, and she gave us multiple prayer requests. We again shared the Gospel with her and left her a Gospel of John with a personal note in the front and a great tip. God answered our prayers and blessed us with a gorgeous, cloud-free day—temps reached eighty-seven degrees! (Sorry—but you need to know what we're experiencing for the Lord.) We returned to my cousin's home for the night, quite content with how the Lord used us today. I can't wait to see who we'll get to minister to tomorrow!

A Better Day than Yesterday!

I never thought we could top what the Lord let us do yesterday, but today it happened. We began our day by going to an old favorite breakfast place called It's All Good! We haven't been there yet this year. We were greeted by a waitress named Dee, who originally was from Queens, New York. We have had her as a server many times over the years, so we have shared the Gospel with her and gave her Gospels of John in the past. We prayed for her again today, and this time, I left the *One Second After You... Die* booklet with a great tip after we prayed for her request.

As we headed north on Route 1, we passed Walker's Honda, and Erik Buell's tractor trailer display was set up in the parking lot. As Ron is a Buell owner, we couldn't pass up stopping to see what they had on display. Ron ended up in a long conversation with the eastern regional sales manager, a man from New Hampshire. He shared the Gospel with him and gave him a Gospel of John. As we were getting ready to leave, a man named Steve came over to talk with me about my Indian. He was originally from Binghamton, New York, and I ended up sharing the Gospel with him before we left for the Speedway.

We then went to the Speedway vendor area to walk through and see what we had missed from the day before. We pulled our bikes right into the vendor area as we did yesterday and walked around for a while. I needed to stop at the Scala Rider booth to get some remedial help in how to use the comm devices Ron and I had on our helmets so we could talk while riding. Then I discovered something! If I parked my bike and just sat on it, people came "from everywhere" to engage in a conversation about the Indian. First, a man named Steve came by, and we talked about the bike. He is from Florida but has moved around quite working in the gambling industry before he retired. I saw an opening, so I asked if I could ask him a personal question. He said, "Sure." I said, "Since you spent your entire career working in the gambling industry, are you going to gamble where you'll spend eternity?" He said, "That doesn't sound like a smart thing to do." We then had a lengthy spiritual discussion. He was raised Catholic but gave up on the religion when he was very young. I took him through the Way of the Master Ten Commandment questions, and he realized that he was going to stand guilty before God… if there was a God. Because he had doubts about God and the Bible, I gave him a *One Second After You… Die* booklet, and he said he would definitely read it. I asked if I could pray for him, and he agreed. I placed my hand on his shoulder, and he put his arm on my back as I prayed. Steve then said that he believed that we met for a reason, and I assured him that this was the case. We met because a sovereign God connected us because He wanted Steve in heaven with Him. Steve wanted my number and e-mail address, so I wrote those in the booklet.

Then a man named John came over to talk about the Indian. He didn't own a motorcycle right now, but his friend just ordered an Indian like mine. He wanted to know how much I liked it, and we talked motorcycles for a while. I asked if I could share something with him as his father walked over. His name is Jim. I shared the Gospel with both of them and gave each of them a Gospel of John to read.

I had parked the Indian right in front of the Scala Rider booth, and both men working the booth were named Mike. Mike (1) helped me get the Scala Rider working with the bike, and Ron came over as I spoke with both Mikes. God arranged, so there were no distractions, and I asked if I could share something with them. We had a wonderful discussion about Christ, and I gave them *One Second After You… Die* booklets. They were very grateful and appreciated what we shared with them.

Ron and I then went north to Rossmeyer's Destination Daytona H-D, the world's largest H-D dealership. We wandered around their campus and ended up in J&P's Cycles store. My leg was bothering me, so I found a bench to sit on while Ron shopped for a seat pad. I laid my helmet on the bench next to me, and a lady came over and asked if she could sit on the bench. I apologized for leaving it on the bench, and she sat down. I asked where she was from, and she said, "San Antonio." She, her husband, and several others rode their bikes to Daytona for the first time. We talked about their trip and ours, and then I asked if she went to church anywhere. She said they were Catholics; and I shared my "hope story" with her and gave her a Gospel of John, which she thanked me for and said she would read. I sat there for quite a while and wondered what happened to Ron. I went looking for him, and he was speaking with a lady named Sue, who was selling the seat pads he was looking for. Apparently, according to Ron, God brought there at exactly the right moment as she said she was a practicing Catholic. I shared my hope story with her, and this lady had an incredible personal story that I don't have the time to write about here. But basically she was wondering why everyone in her family had died and left her here, and she was wondering why she was still here. We explained that God kept her here so she could meet Ron and me, because God wanted her in heaven with Him when she died. He sent us to tell her how to make that decision. We shared a Gospel of John with her and clearly spelled out the plan of salvation. I also gave her a YouTube video link to check out that would clearly explain what we had shared with her.

We then left and head back to Daytona, stopping at Chick-fil-A for dinner. We had a young lady named Kentrice serve us at the counter. We had a nice discussion with her, and she was a sweetheart. We asked if we could pray for her, and she told us she was a senior in high school and was studying very had for the upcoming SAT and ACT tests for college. We prayed for her. I wrote a nice note to her in a Gospel of John and brought it up to her at the counter. I explained what it was, and she was overwhelmed by what we had done for her. All of the girls behind the counter gathered around her, and they read the note I wrote. After her coworkers moved away, she continued reading it as I watched from the table.

Praise God for an incredible day with beautiful weather and divine appointments!

Today's Ministry

This morning, we went to C's Waffles for breakfast and had the opportunity to pray for and share a Gospel of John with our waitress

Alexis. When we went out to the bikes, a crowd of retirees appeared almost out of nowhere to look at the Indian and ask questions. My former good friend Ron offered to let them take my bike for a ride. Thanks, pal… Ron passed out Gospels of John to many of them, and we headed to the Indian dealership for an appointment to have my clutch adjusted.

We walked across the street to meet Pete from Butt Buffer. I had mailed him a six-CD set by Chip Ingram called "Why I Believe." Pete told me he would listen to it on his ride from Pennsylvania to Florida. I asked Pete if he had listened to them, and sadly, he told me that he started to but couldn't listen past the first five to six minutes because he wanted nothing to do with what he heard. I spoke with him about giving them a chance before making a decision, and he refused. Ron also tried to encourage him, but we made no progress. His eternity is in the Lord's hands…nothing more we can do other than pray.

Ron and I walked among the vendors on Beach Street while the dealership worked on the bike; and we met a nice entrepreneur named Bill, who was previewing an airbag product he had developed for protect motorcycles as they were being transported in trailers. We talked for quite a while, and I shared a Gospel of John with him; and I asked if we could pray for him, his family, and the success of his business venture. He gladly agreed, so Ron and I laid hands on him and prayed for him. He was so grateful for what we did for him.

As we walked along, I saw the booth of Michele Smith, the lady who hosted the TV program *American Thunder* for ten years. This was by far my favorite motorcycle show on TV. There was no one else around, and we talked for quite a while. She was born and raised in Harrisburg, Pennsylvania, and lived in Los Angeles doing modeling and hosting the show. When the show went off the air, she moved to Florida and has a lingerie line that she sells to make a living. She also does public appearances at motorcycle events around the country. I asked if I could share something with her, and she said it was okay. So I gave her a *One Second After You… Die* booklet and explained what it was about, and she agreed to take it and read it.

When I went back to pick up the motorcycle, I had the opportunity to interact with several more people. I met a man named Rick from St. Louis. He and a friend rode 1,300 miles in two days to get to Daytona. On the way here, in Mississippi, his buddy was leading in the rain at about sixty miles per hour, when a large beagle crossed right in front of him. He hit the poor dog at almost sixty and went down on the bike. As the road was wet, he slide a long way but only ended up with a little road rash and a slight cut on one finger. Talk about a miracle! Rick showed me pix of the bike and the crash scene. The Victory Vision motorcycle was clearly totaled as it flipped over and over, and Rick's friend was upstairs signing papers for the purchase of a new Victory Cross Country Tour. Then I had a chance to speak with the mechanic who worked on my bike. He is from Columbia, New Jersey, right near the Delaware Water Gap! We talked for a while, and then Ron and I headed out and rode the scenic loop.

At dinner, we had a waitress named Nadia. We were able to share the Gospel and pray for her. While we were waiting for our meal, a *very* big man was escorted to a booth adjacent to our table. He looked at the menu and placed his order with Nadia. The Holy Spirit kept telling me to invite him to sit with us. So I did. He said he was waiting for a friend, so he thanked me and continued to wait. We continued to talk even though he wasn't sitting right with us. His name is Greg, and he is working on repainting the Capitol in Washington! He pulled out his phone and showed us some incredible photos that most people never get to see. He had photos he had taken from the roof of the capital looking in different directions. He even had photos of the National Christmas Tree being put up and a shot of it all lit up at night. We had a great time speaking with him, and I shared a Gospel of John with him before we left. I told Ron that there were a group of Israeli motorcycle riders sitting behind him. The one man had a shirt that had a set of wings on the back with the Star of David in the middle. Above this is "The 13th Tribe." Ron turned around and went over to them to speak with them. They told him they were the "lost" tribe.

God blessed us with another beautiful day to minister in. We are grateful to Him for his provision and blessing! Tomorrow Ron is headed to Ocala to meet with some old friends. I plan on parking my bike at the Speedway and sitting on it, expecting a large group of people to come and talk with me about the bike. Then I will talk about Jesus. Prayers appreciated!

Different Day Today

We had an interesting day today. Ron and I had breakfast together and prayed for Marisol, our waitress. We wrote her a nice note in the cover of the Gospel of John that we left her. Ron then headed an hour and a half away to Ocala to visit some old friends for lunch. I went to the Speedway vendor area. I found a nice spot on a corner and was able to get in the shade of a large tent for most of the morning. I sat with my Indian, and as people came by and showed interest in the bike, we talked about it, and I shared when the opportunity arose.

I was amazed at how many Christian ministries had a presence at the Speedway. I've never seen this many different organizations at Bike Week. There were a number of booths where they were pulling people in to share Christ with them. Some of these groups offered the opportunity to enter their names in a drawing for a new motorcycle if they listened to a three-minute Gospel presentation. They would then pray for the people and turn them loose with some tracts. I spoke with a number of my brothers and sisters in the Lord who were there to minister and gave out quite a few business cards to these people who were from all over the southern US. Lord willing some new doors of ministry will open for us.

One pastor at a booth and I had a nice discussion, and he told me what their goals were in terms of how many salvations they wanted to see at Bike Week. He asked me what my goal was, and I told him that my goal was to be faithful to share Christ with the people God connected me with and to leave the results to Him. He kept pressuring me to give him a number, and I told him that I had no number because it's not up to me. I have no control over how many people give their lives to Christ... That was God's job. Mine was simply to share the good news with the people I connected with, and it was up to God to cause the growth. The conversation was disturbing. I don't believe that all of the Christian organizations that were there to minister had the same mentality and plan, but this one sure did. I mentioned to the pastor that no one ever got saved in the Bible by praying a prayer, and if that was his goal, then he was just creating false converts. He seemed surprised by what I said.

It was *very* hot and humid all morning, and at about one o'clock, I needed a drink. So I got on the bike and rode over to Chick-fil-A for some refreshment. I spoke with a number of people inside and outside and met a group of Christian school students from Miami who were on their way to a competition in Jacksonville. I shared our ministry with two of the leaders and gave them my card. They expressed some interest in having me do some ministry at the school at some point in the future. Then my abdomen started to bother me, and I knew I had to get back to the house as something I had eaten was not agreeing with me. I made it back just in time (sorry... I know... TMI) and felt like I should stay at the house for the afternoon because I still felt a little weird.

Ron called at 5:30 p.m. and said he was just leaving Ocala... Time had gotten away from him, and he was headed back to Daytona. Judy and Keith had a nice meal for us for dinner, and we are calling it a day. One more day tomorrow to see whom we'll get to share with. Thanks for your prayers!

Ministry on Our Last Day in Daytona

Ron and I went to C's Waffles for breakfast again today. We had a waitress named Kathy. She looked familiar to us, and Ron figured out who she was. She was our waitress a number of years ago at It's All Good in Port Orange, where we used to go for breakfast. She is now working at C's. As soon as he said that, I remembered her. We would go there every day for breakfast, and we got a different waitress every day. As usual, we offered to pray for our waitresses, and we left a Gospel of John for them with a nice note in the front. On our last day in the area, a waitress that we had before told us that Kathy was disappointed as she was the only one who hadn't received a Gospel with a note written in front. So I pulled out another Gospel, wrote her a note, and approached her as she stood at the kitchen serving window. As I walked up to her, she kind of smiled, and I reiterated what was told to me. I presented her with the Gospel of John, and I told her that I wanted to pray for her as well. She stammered and said, "Right here...right now"? I said, "Yes. Right here and right now. How can I pray for you today?" She gave me a request, and I put my hand on her shoulder and prayer for her as she stood there. It seemed like every eye in the restaurant was on us. She hugged me and thanked me, and we left.

Kathy remembered us when Ron mentioned the other restaurant, and she was very glad to see us again. Today we prayed for her, and this time I left her a *One Second After You... Die* booklet with a nice note in the front.

Ron and I then headed to the Speedway to test drive some motorcycles. I got to share with a number of people as we waited for our turn to ride. One man was from southern New Jersey. He is a Catholic, and his name is Wayne. As we talked, Ron saw an opening and turned the conversation, and I finished it with him because of my background. I also spoke with a man named Mike.

As I was waiting for Ron to gas up at a Sunoco station on International Speedway Boulevard, a nice Honda motorcycle pulled up and stopped next to me. It definitely had some custom work done on it. The lady got off the passenger seat and commented on how much she liked my Indian. Her husband and I got into a discussion about the bike, and I asked their names. They were Mike and Janet Jackson. Yep... Janet Jackson. As we finished our motorcycle conversation, I pulled a Gospel of John out of my pocket and explained it to them. They said they attended a church in Georgia, and I quickly just confirmed that they had indeed surrendered to Christ in repentance and faith. They affirmed that they had, so I took them at their word (after planting a quick seed), and I suggested they keep the Gospel and share it with someone they come in contact with.

I ended up back in the Scala Rider booth to have them help with some of the tech questions and issues I had been experiencing. After getting the problems resolved, I spoke with the two Mikes about the booklet I had given them and encouraged them to read it and let me know if they had any questions. They both agreed that they would contact me after reading it.

We took my cousin by marriage and his wife out for dinner to thank them for letting us stay with them. We prayed for our server named Randy and his son who had just called him about the steel belts coming through his tire. Randy asked us to pray that they would arrive at the Firestone dealer safely. After we prayed, Randy stopped back, thanked us, and told us his son had arrived at the Firestone dealership and was having the tire replaced. As we were eating, I saw a sheriff's deputy walk in and get seated. I felt his urge to go and share the Gospel with him. As I approached his table, I saw him bow his head and ask a blessing on his meal. I waited until he had finished, introduced myself to him, and told him I was coming over to share Christ with him. He smiled and said I was too late. He already was a follower of Jesus. We talked for a while about the frustrations and struggles he's facing on the job, and I went back to my table. Again, I felt the prompting to go and speak with him, and this time I felt that I needed to pray for him. So I returned to his table and asked if I could pray for him. He smiled and agreed. I laid my hand on his shoulder, he bowed his head, and I prayed God's blessing and protection on him and his family and that God would grant him discernment and discretion as he deals with the dangerous situations he finds himself in. He thanked me and I left.

As we reflect on what God had lined up for us down here, we are grateful for the privilege of serving Him. These trips always give us a "shot in the arm" and get us refocused on what we're here to do. The trip also gives me fresh new stories to share as I teach the MAD Live event.

Tomorrow we'll be heading back to Columbia—four hundred-plus miles. I know God has additional divine appointments planned for us as we travel north. We look forward to whom we'll get to meet as we continue home. Please pray for safety and good weather for us.

Heading North

We began our trek home today at 7:15 a.m., stopping just north of Jacksonville for breakfast. We had a nice waitress named Heather, whom we prayed for. I forgot that I had left my phone in the saddlebag, so I went out to get it. Guess what happened—another divine appointment at the Indian. A man walked up to me and started asking questions about the Indian. His name is Carter, and he is from the Upper Peninsula of Michigan. He owns four Harleys and a Cobra sports car. We talked about motorcycles for a bit, and then I asked if I could share something with him. He said, "Sure!" I pulled out a Gospel of John and explained what it was and that he would be dying someday and going to someplace for eternity. He said he expected it to happen sometime soon, as he was seventy-seven years old. Wow. We talked a little more about the Lord, and he thanked me over and over again for the Gospel and said he would definitely read it and take the contents to heart. Praise the Lord!

Ron and I stopped in Georgia just before the South Carolina line to get gas. Being the forecast north of us was for rain, we opted to don our rain gear in the safety of the convenience store parking lot. That's a whole lot better than doing it on the side of the highway. God is good, because as soon as we entered the highway from the on ramp, the rain started. We were in and out of rain for the next 155 miles until we arrived at the Burnett household in West Columbia where the truck and trailer had been parked. Unfortunately, the family was going through a *very* nasty stomach bug, and we thought it best not to spend the night there as planned. So we packed up the bikes and gear and headed north, arriving in Wytheville, Virginia, for the night. Along the way, we stopped for dinner and prayed for our waitress named Bri, leaving her a note in the front of the *One Second After You... Die* booklet and a great tip.

Thanks for our prayer for safety. God definitely honored and answered them. We should be home tomorrow!

Divine Appointment at the Bus Garage

I have been helping a local school district driving a school bus for them in the mornings, as they are desperate for drivers. The run I have is one no one wants. I drive the "troubled teens" to a special county school where I can't let them off the bus until and escort comes out. As they enter the school, they pass through a metal detector and then are "wanded" to be sure they have no weapons. I was doing my pretrip bus check when the lady named Donna, who drives the bus parked next to me, asked if I wanted her to check my brake lights and backup lights. I said, "Sure." After checking the lights, I exited the bus, and we talked. She asked me how I liked driving these kids to school, and I told her it really wasn't that big of a deal. I told her that the other day one of the teens got on the bus, and he reeked of marijuana. When the escort at the school came out to get the kids, he immediately smelled it and asked me which student it was, and I told him. The student hasn't been on the bus since. I was told he had to meet with his probation officer for a drug test and that he may be locked up now. Donna told me that she has never smelled marijuana and has no idea what it smells like. I described it as best I could, and then she said that when here kids were growing up, she doubts they ever used drugs, but they probably drank. I told her that I had never smoked, drank, or taken drugs. She said, "Wow, so you'll live forever!" Open door… I told her that everyone was going to live forever; the only question was where we will be spending eternity. She asked if that meant that we would be "coming back to life." I explained what was going to happen and shared the Gospel with her using the "Way of the Master" questions. Donna told me that her fiancé died six months ago and that she has not been able to move on with her life since then. I explained how Jesus could change all of that and gave her a copy of *One Second After You… Die*, and she thanked me repeatedly and said she would read it and get back to me with questions. Donna then made the comment that we must have met for a reason. I told her that God brought me to the school district and had me drive the bus parked next to hers so we could meet. God wants Donna in heaven with him when she dies.

I look forward to following up with her tomorrow morning. Pray for Donna!

*****

Friday, I was blessed to be able to share the Gospel with four people. Yesterday, there were two. Today I went for a motorcycle ride with my friend John. Of course, John had an ice cream stop planned. I was sitting at a picnic table with my back to the Indian; and a guy walked over, looked at the motorcycle, and commented how beautiful the bike is. He asked if I minded telling him how much it cost. I got up and had a nice discussion with him about the Indian and its features. He and his wife were riding an H-D. After the motorcycle conversation was at end, I asked if I could share something with him. I reached into my saddlebag, pulled out a Gospel of John with the plan of salvation in it, and explained it to him. He said that he has a tough life physically...a heart attack that resulted in him coding three times before they brought him back. He shattered a disk in his spine and had to have it replaced with a synthetic one. He showed me the scar on the front of his neck where they went on to fix it. Now he has to go in for hip surgery! I asked if I could pray for him, and he said, "Yes...please do!" I laid hands on him and prayed for his healing and a quick return to some type of a normal life. After finishing the prayer, I commented that God spared him when he coded so he could meet me today, because God really wants Chris and his wife, Kelly, in heaven with Him. He said he believes that and thanked me for praying for him and sharing the Gospel with him. God is good!

ABOUT THE AUTHOR

Don is not your typical church speaker, having no seminary or Bible college degree. He is a lay person in full-time vocational service for Christ. He and his wife Cathy attended premarital counseling at his future mother-in-law's church (the North Caldwell C&MA), and Don and Cathy were confronted with the truths of the gospel. That night, Cathy and Don made individual decisions to repent and trust Jesus Christ with their eternal salvation. They followed our Lord in believer's baptism and were married in June of 1973.

Don served as a police officer in northern New Jersey for about four years and a deputy game warden in Pennsylvania for nine years. He was also privileged to attend SWAT training at the FBI Academy in Quantico, Virginia, and served on the department SWAT team for the duration of his employment. The Lord eventually led Don out of police work and into the computer and software industry where he held various sales and management positions for twenty-four years with companies like Apple and AT&T. In the fall of 2004, God called Don and Cathy into full-time ministry at Family Life Ministries in Bath, New York. While there, Don created the Make a Difference material and began teaching followers of Jesus Christ how to share their faith as a lifestyle and make disciples. He has taught his Make a Difference training over six hundred times to people in 35 states and several foreign countries.

Don and Cathy have two grown married children (Jaimie and John) and are blessed with seven grandchildren. Don's hobbies include motorcycle and ATV riding and touring, hunting, and woodworking.

CPSIA information can be obtained
at www.ICGtesting.com
Printed in the USA
LVHW101754221022
731289LV00001B/5